FUTURE TRIBES
HEYNIEK

OTHER WORLDLY

FOREWORD

by
GREG FRENCH

On the otherworldly in fashion and the role of fantasy in the revolution of everyday life.

What is the otherworldly? It seems only appropriate to begin with that question, even if we may not be able to conclude with an answer. After all, the concept is informed by the unknown or the unexplainable. For something to be otherworldly, its content or context must be unbound by earthly constraints. It is a space for fantasy and a place for dreams.

Fashion, with its propensity for playing with fantasy and making dreams into reality, is a sort of gateway for immersing ourselves in the idea of the otherworldly. From the repetitive weaving of the designer's needle to the acute precision of a 3D printer, and from the flash of the photographer's bulb to the pixel rendered on a digital display, fashion transforms our naked bodies, pages, and screens into something other than their most basic forms. These transformations are the otherworldly results of this-worldly processes. This book examines moments in which such an approach is placed center stage in an attempt to demystify this often hazy yet pioneering area of dress.

This moment in the twenty-first century is an appropriate time for such scrutiny—particularly because of the way our era has played with concepts of the postmodern. Fashion has finally been handed the capabilities, thanks to the rise of new digital technologies, with which to bring to life the often dreamlike and seemingly unattainable musings of its creators. The internet provides an arena in which designers can realize whatever creations their 3D printers and alternative materials are still incapable of materializing. It offers an opportunity to play the role of Dr. Frankenstein—or even the role of Frankenstein's monster itself. Ultimately, we as a civilization are entering a time that can be classified as post-human, where the very fabric of our DNA is changing. Gender has become little more than a social construct, robotics can replace or enhance our own weakening limbs, and drones now fly side-by-side with birds in our skies.

And yet, the moment in which we currently find ourselves is not a point of departure from the general course that we have traveled thus far. Fashion has interacted with the idea of the otherworldly throughout history. There have always been icons who lived their lives dressed like apparitions from another world, like Marchesa Luisa Casati of the Belle Époque era, who would roam the canals of Venice on a gondola with whitened skin, kohl black eyes, and fiery red hair alongside her bejewelled pet cheetahs and white peacocks. This interaction between fashion and the otherworldly can be seen most clearly in times of great subcultural revolution. The desire to change that which is, is an inherent part of the human psyche. Acting on that desire is a necessary step in the evolution of our species.

The individual, the outsider, the pioneer, and the mutant: these are the characters who so frequently lead that mutiny. And because of the visual nature of the fashion industry, their contributions are especially visible. As Elsa Schiaparelli once said, "In difficult times, fashion is always outrageous."

Indeed, Schiaparelli herself was considered an "outrageous" designer herself on the basis of her much-replicated skeleton dress and her use of optical illusions. Her simple introduction of shocking pink to the palette of a world where women so often favored monotonous clothes was enough to lift fashion out of the drudgery of a war-torn world. This is just one example of fashion's power to alter the reality in which we live.

The musician Grace Jones may be one of the best examples of the application of that reality-altering power. Her constant reinvention of herself is a testament to the metamorphic nature inherent to fashion. Her androgynous features, most notably her shaved head, were to garner attention among the international fashion community. Jones exemplifies the use of fashion to forge a look in total rebellion against those around you—her hair itself was a revolt against the strict religious atmosphere of her family life. "One creates oneself," as she said. "Art and illusion are supposed to be fantasy."

From Mugler to McQueen, and from Bowie to Bowery, we have seen milestone figures champion this notion of advancing or transforming society through design in their own explosive ways. Yet, more importantly, these pioneers have also set in motion a ripple effect that has seen artists and designers at varying levels produce some astonishing bodies of work while providing subject matter for some of our most idiosyncratic image-makers. Olivier Theyskens' early work in the late 1990s employed plumes of dismembered bird wings swarmed around masked models to give the appearance of fantasy through *mis-en-scene.* Aitor Throup Studio has generated clothing from concept drawings, cloaked models beneath skeletal headgear, and deployed tech-spec trousers to create a utilitarian army of the future. Vetements and Craig Green play with distortions of the human body through proportion or abstract adornment, spawning a look that recodes the human silhouette. Often these designs toe a fine line between clothing and costume, sometimes poised so ambiguously between the two that it becomes difficult to distinguish the act of wearing them from performance art.

A costume, by its nature, is designed to change or enhance the identity of its wearer. In stepping into a costume, you commit yourself to being something other than the character you play each day. It is a transformation capable of changing the mannerisms of the wearer, granting them access to an entirely different life. This may be why extreme fashion choices, which often play with the characteristics of costume, are so frequently adapted by radical individuals in their attempts to challenge the establishment of everyday life.

This approach was perhaps most notably seen in the 1980s and 1990s, when club-kid culture catalyzed a scene where these creative practices merged together, becoming a melting pot for anarchistic schools of thought. In the cities of London and New York, which at the time were beset by economic depression and political unrest, creatives sought to forge their own worlds as a form of escapism. Avant-garde dress was every bit as important as music, drugs, and alcohol in enabling them to escape from this world and create another.

The subculture's dependence on fantasy can be seen in the theater, film, and art of that time. Due to fashion's ability to convey the otherworldly, it became the current that would run through them all. For instance, the last decade of the twentieth century saw the release of Matthew Barney's *The Cremaster Cycle*—a series of five feature-length films that explored concepts of embryonic gender development. The films play out across a series of transcendental worlds and features mythical characters who control the progression of the plot. Their costumes frequently borrow from the land of club-kid dress, with assistance from iconic designers like Isaac Mizrahi, Manolo Blahnik, and Prada, and input from MAC Cosmetics and Vidal Sassoon. The same can be said for dystopian movies like *The Fifth Element,* whose costume designer was Jean Paul Gaultier, or Tarsem Singh's *The Cell,* which saw designer Eiko Ishioka produce spectacular clothing that relayed the fantastical musings of a serial killer's mind.

Why and how, then, have these extremities of otherworldly fashion come about? What explains this cultural phenomenon and the steps leading up to it? The work of Cypriot artist Alexis Themistocleous may help us find the answer. Daubed in black face paint, diamond-encrusted ski masks, or restrictive suiting, Themistocleous was able to mask his true identity and forge an entirely new creature altogether. This character was then captured through film, photography, and 3D scanning. The glitchy nature of these mediums was used to heighten the enigmatic nature of the strange new being. Out of this imagery he created an online profile, achieving a kind of existence for his alter ego that takes Grace Jones' notion of creating oneself to an entirely new dimension.

Themistocleous further developed this idea in 2012 when he took the character he had created out of the realm of the internet and began living it in real life. Fashion equipped him with the ability to do so by his use of props, headpieces, and garments to alter his appearance. But the exercise did not stop there: Themistocleous created not only costumes but also his own currency, all while creatively hijacking galleries and wall spaces around the world. He even graced the cover of the fashion magazine *Dazed & Confused,* a nod to how easy it has become to completely mutate oneself. He christened his new identity Theo-Mass Lexileictous, an anagram of his own name that roughly translates to "god of the masses." It is this character who is the editor of this book.

The ability to realize such otherworldly ambitions on such a scale may be new, but the impulse is not. The writings of the Situationist Guy Debord may help make sense of the phenomenon. His work, especially his 1967 text

Society of the Spectacle, examines a world that has become mediated by imagery of the spectacular. He argues, "everything that was directly lived has moved away into a representation." This is true for the otherworldly in fashion—when the world has become so dehumanized, as in Theo-Mass' case, an entirely new fantasy world can be created. This, in essence, is why fashion is so important as a revolutionary tool and why it has the ability to challenge societal conventions. Debord says, "images detached from every aspect of life fuse in a common stream in which the unity of this life can no longer be re-established. Reality considered partially unfolds…" Ultimately, Debord's writing suggests that the more spectacular the image, the further it is from reality itself and the more otherworldly it becomes.

Clothing complicates this idea though, for no matter how extravagantly we dress, beneath the layers of garments lies the essence of the terrestrial: our bodies. The imagery created for fashion—particularly photography of which you will find many examples in this book—creates a space where the otherworldly can be most clearly explored. A selection of fashion photographers and image-makers have delved deep into the realm of the otherworldly, creating fictitious sets, computer-generated anthropomorphic aliens, and impossible narratives. This approach can be traced back to some of the earliest fashion photographers, like Erwin Blumenfeld, who used smoke and mirrors to create the illusion of celestial beings bound not to reality, but rather to the black ether on which they were shot. Likewise, Guy Bourdin used the Polaroid, an artistic form known for instantly capturing that which can be seen, to present unearthly stills, which were often devoid of complete bodily forms or obscured in ways that created a sinister presence. Mert & Marcus, Tim Walker, and Steven Klein also explored these techniques, conjuring up mythical landscapes in which their macabre and inhuman figures found solace.

The rendered pixel has become the new home of the otherworldly, able to change its form and function within a split second. Technology has given us new ways of creating as well as new ways of seeing, and the work of Nick Knight is a testament to that. "Now we have a number of wonderful apps and the ability to do whatever we want with an image," he once told me. "Now it's different processes, different chemicals—based on phosphorous on a screen. I can make a 3D object out of anything with the press of a button."

For Tokyo retail giant Lane Crawford's spring/summer 2013 campaign, Knight used 3D scanning software to record four of the season's looks on model Ming Xi. The resulting render was then combined with animation and digitally manipulated so that the walking model would shatter into a thousand fragmented pixels, reducing the mutated human body to nothing less than a swirling geometric dust cloud. The effect elevated the character, distancing it from the truth-capturing capabilities of the conventional video camera. The resulting figures were transported out of the confines of reality by fashion.

But it is not just within fashion imagery that we have seen the effects of the digital revolution. Technology has equipped us with the ability to live out some of our fictitious fantasies in the real world, morphing the capabilities of the human body into something superhuman. Military research, which often has the end game of producing soldiers who are stronger, faster, and less susceptible to fatigue or health risks, has seen the production of third-generation robotic suits capable of doing just that. We also now have living fabrics that react to weather conditions or perspiration, mechanical dogs whose piston legs are capable of jumping to inhuman heights, and even prosthetic limbs that enable Paralympic athletes to compete in their disciplines once again.

Aimee Mullins is one such athlete—at once otherworldly and yet very, very real. The double-amputee also starred in the aforementioned *The Cremaster Cycle,* portraying six different fantastical characters, and appeared on the cover of *Dazed & Confused.* Her appearances question the role and responsibility of fashion within the wider world. Mullins's disability was celebrated in Alexander McQueen's spring/summer 1999 show, for which the designer and his team carved an exquisitely detailed prosthetic leg out of elm wood for Mullins. In doing so, Mullins passed unnoticed amongst the other models around her, subverting expectations about her condition. "I made a point of not putting her in sprinting legs. We did try them on, but I thought no, that's not the point of this exercise," commented McQueen after the show. "The point is that she would mold in with the rest of the girls."

The idea of the otherworldly in fashion provides us with a passage through which we can transport ourselves into partial or even complete fantasy. At one end of the spectrum, that may mean immersing ourselves in a spectacular runway show; at the other, it could mean using fashion's transformative power to forge an entirely new character altogether. Once we are there, we can subvert the socio-political hierarchies of the everyday and the reality in which they are grounded. As Debord and the Situationists suggested, we are now able to live our lives almost entirely within an alternate reality that is constructed solely by the individual. That is why, in the spirit of Schiaparelli, we can be sure that fashion itself will thrive and help us to evolve as terrestrial beings, even, or especially, in times of great instability. That is what makes the otherworldly so very important: it helps us make a version of the world that we can have an impact on.

And now, at the end, we return the beginning. What is the otherworldly? It is a tool—a powerful tool for radically altering the world we see around us. The pages of this book will show you how it can be used to create new ways to see and to live—and the fantastic people responsible for remaking our realities.

IIMUAHII

BEA SZENFELD

PORTRAIT

The work of BEA SZENFELD **explores the visual identity of mythical creatures and uses unconventional materials in order to challenge various entrenched ideas surrounding classical notions of design and dress. Born in Poland in 1972, the designer studied at Beckmans College of Design in Stockholm, Sweden, before going on to open her own label.**

The designer has worked with the likes of Swarovski, Tommy Hilfiger, Hello Kitty, and Stella McCartney, winning an internship with the latter after beating out British designer Gareth Pugh.

The medium of paper is used throughout her wide-ranging designs, replacing the normative use of fabric and needle. Her spring/summer 2014 collection "Haute Papier" featured gigantic origami structures, layered and folded like suits of armor, that were meant to drape over the body and shoulders. She formed geometric shapes out of meticulously folded paper—bleached, colored, and in-stitched—that created a new scale-like texture that looked every bit fragile as it did durable.

Her material-minded use of paper itself holds particular significance in her collection "Sur le Plage" (or "From the Sea"). In this collection, bathing suits are made up of hundreds of disks of paper, glued together to reference the flesh and skin of ocean-bound creatures. The hand-constructed pieces are delicate, and, ironically, the same underwater world that inspired the bathing suits would also destroy them if they were ever exposed to it.

Her designs radically alter the overall silhouette of the human body, producing wearable sculptures whose large structures encapsulate and cocoon the naked human body. While paper may not be seen as a durable fabric, Szenfeld's manipulation of it proves otherwise. Rejecting the use of cutting machines or 3D printers, the craftsmanship with which she produces these pieces is breathtaking and a true testament to her creative vision and execution.

As a result, her work has earned her an international reputation as a designer whose collections are both playful and cutting-edge. Her creations have graced the likes of Lady Gaga and Björk. The latter has even worn pieces from the designer's collections to award ceremonies and, in 2010, she exhibited them on the front cover of *AnOther Magazine.*

At the heart of Bea Szenfeld's impressive creations is the notion of metamorphosis. Whether arising from her transmutations of paper into architectural forms, her interrogations of forms of bodily protection, or her fictitious amphibians from which she draws inspiration, her work is a radically new approach to fashion design—a field that she believes is the easiest method of communication.

HAUTE
PAPIER

SUR
LA PLAGE

FREDERIK
HEYMAN

V.I.T.R.I.O.L

VASISTAS
by

JULIEN
PALMILHA

ONLY ANGELS HAVE WINGS

NIKOLINE
LIV ANDERSEN

TANEL
VEENRE

DINO BODICIU

SPECIMEN

PETER POPPS

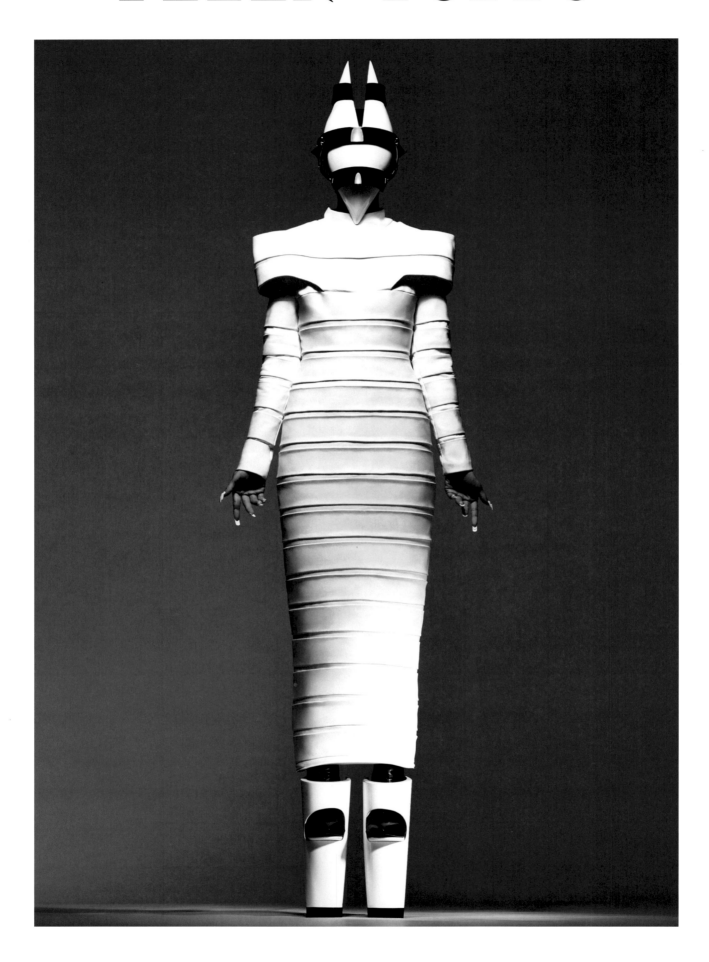

THE CONE

THE SWING

SELFPORTRAIT

THE PLANETARY ALIGNMENT

THEO-MASS
LEXILEICTOUS

BLOCK BUSTES
by

HEYNIEK

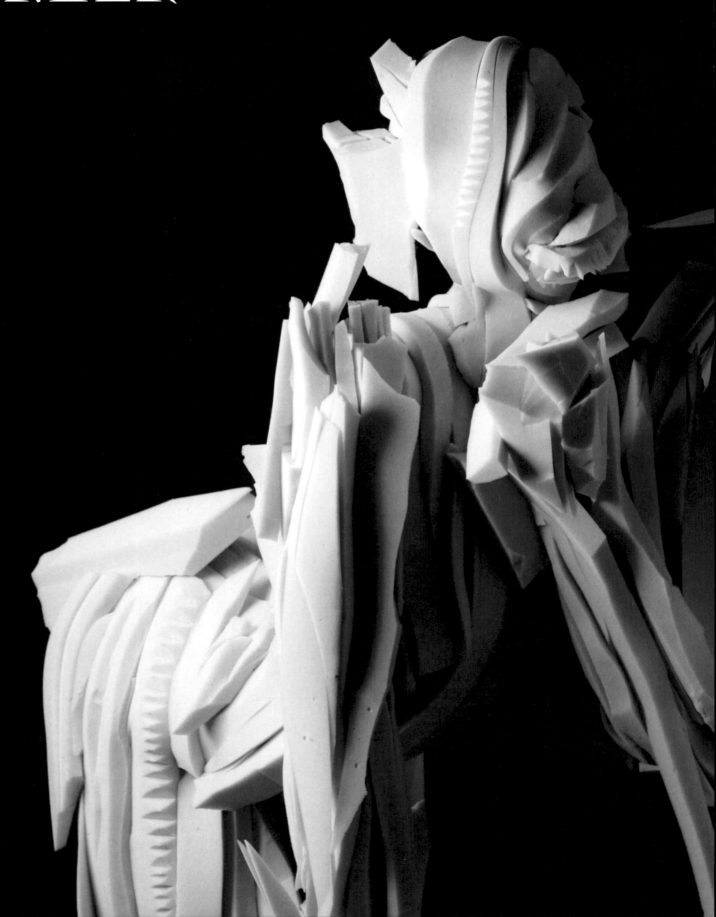

LES PLEURS

JULIEN
PALMILHA

REIN
VOLLENGA

ALEXANDER
STRAULINO

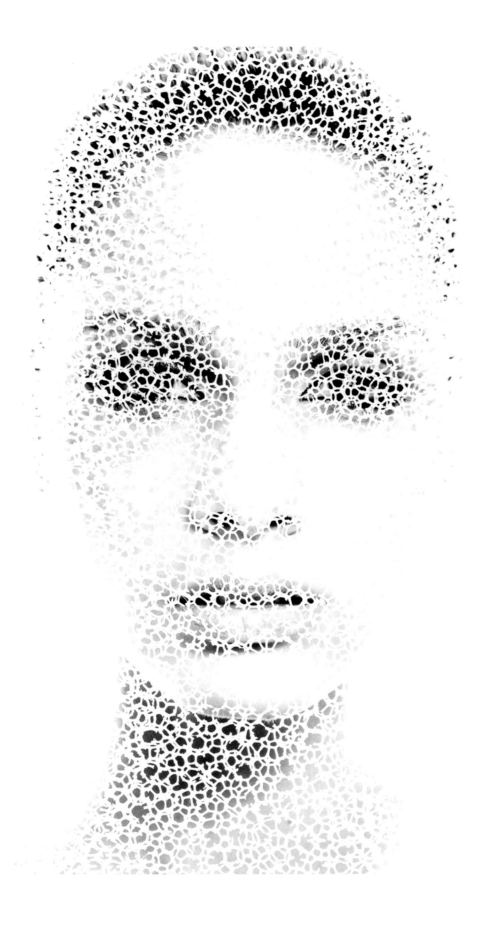

IRIS VAN HERPEN

PORTRAIT

IRIS VAN HERPEN is credited as perhaps one of the most pioneering designers of the twenty-first century. Her work is inspired by nature and technology, but most importantly by the chasm that exists between these two opposing constructs. Van Herpen's work champions new technologies that give her the ability to play god, creating forms that would otherwise take hundreds of years to produce.

Initially trained in ballet, van Herpen took an interest in the moving body from a very early age. This would grow into her love of fashion, in which the moving body becomes a frame on which to display her creations. This interaction between the human figure and the fantastical works of art that she produces is what defines the aesthetic of her eponymous label.

The term "work of art" is indeed applicable to the Dutch fashion designer's creations, as her designs hover precariously between haute couture, ready to wear, and performance. From layers of vinyl that protect the body as though they were armadillo skin to 3D printed skeletal frames that hang louchely over the body, it is clear that van Herpen's creations are not necessarily made to be worn in the everyday world.
Van Herpen was educated in fashion design at the ArtEZ Institute of the Arts in the Netherlands before going on to work with the likes of Alexander McQueen and Claudy Jongstra, whose concepts of spectacle had a visual influence on the work that she would later produce. In 2007, she started her own design house, which from the start exhibited an obvious enthusiasm for technology and collaboration.

This love of collaboration is central to the work she produces: she prefers to work as part of a team rather than as a solitary design figure. Through her collaborations she has been able to push fabrication and form to their absolute limits by utilizing partners working outside the sphere of fashion. She has included everyone from architects to biochemists in her attempt to challenge the foundations of design and production. Her 2013 collection "Hybrid Holism" offers substantial insight into this approach, which saw van Herpen team up with architect Philip Beesley to explore responsive design by experimenting with living structures and spaces that can change according to the conditions to which they are exposed. It is here that fashion becomes much more than just a piece of clothing, manifesting instead as something that can change the way we live our day-to-day lives.

For this reason, van Herpen is not interested in mass production. Her work is uniquely complex and uniquely time-consuming; she fervently rejects the fast-paced nature of our modern-day fashion system. Rather, she champions the idea of materiality and shortening the gap between designer and consumer. In her eyes, 3D printing and technology are possible means to this end—and tools for an emerging future where consumers will be able to print the clothes they want at home.

Fittingly, she describes her atelier as a kind of laboratory, a place where she can discover new ways of working and producing in order to recode our approach to fashion design.

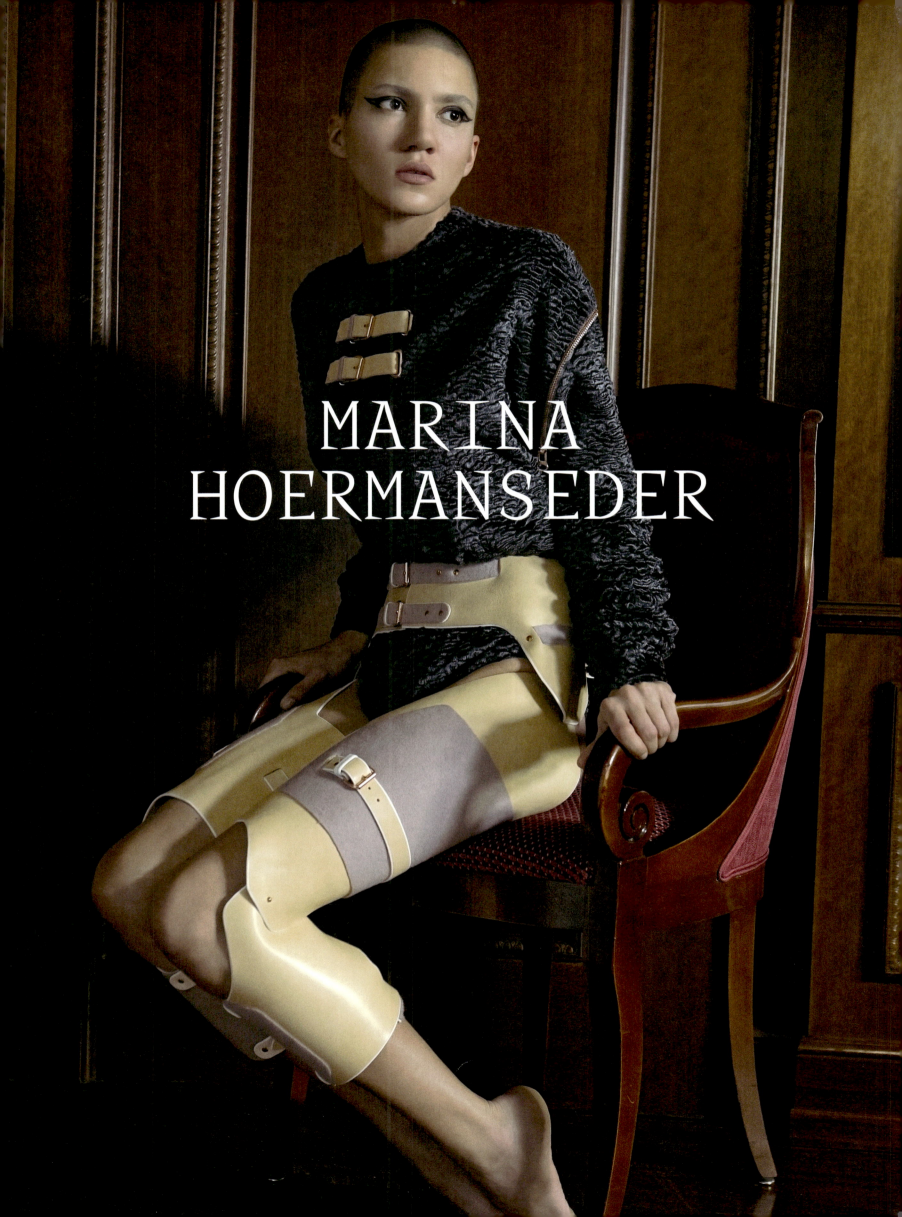

MARINA
HOERMANSEDER

ANIMAL:

THE OTHER SIDE OF EVOLUTION

by

ANA RAJCEVIC

PATRICK IAN HARTLEY

GLIMM RUBEUS

RE.TREAT

by

ÚNA BURKE

MIODRAG GUBERINIC

TETRA

THEO-MASS LEXILEICTOUS

EXTRATERRESTRIAL

DANIEL

SANNWALD

HOOD

JANE BOWLER

NEKROMANTIK by
KATARINA
KONIECZKA

THREE AS FOUR

AIR

IRENE
BUSSEMAKER

HYUNGKOO
LEE

THE
OBJECTUALS

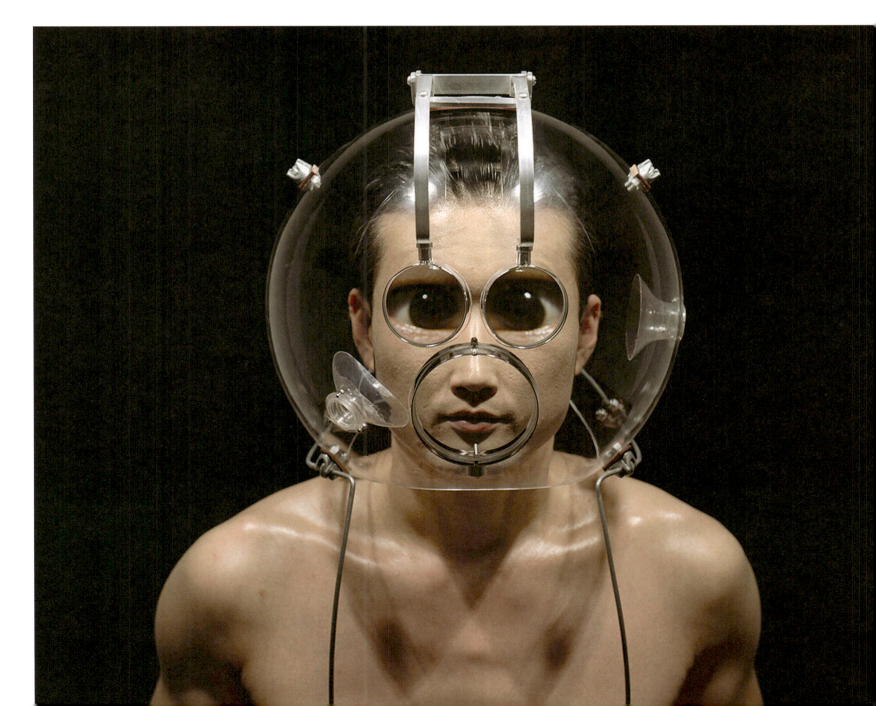

BIRTH
OF THE NEW

HOW DESIGNERS ARE USING MUTATION TO
REINVENT THE BODY, REFASHION THE
MATERIALS THAT CLOTHE IT, AND EVEN
REIMAGINE WHAT IT MEANS TO BE HUMAN.

HEYNIEK

by THEO-MASS LEXILEICTOUS
BODY

Mutation, with its combination of questioning and creating, makes it a fascinating object of exploration for creators and audiences alike, and the attention it has attracted from the press has established it as one of the greatest phenomena in the fashion industry.

The term mutation usually refers to a complete change of form, structure, or substance—a transformation on all levels. Genetic mutation is a permanent alteration in the DNA sequence that makes up a gene. It creates different versions of the same genes and can result in alterations and variations in physical appearance, facial structure, skin color, height, body shape, and behavior.

Fashion provides an alternate method for producing such mutations: temporary and designed, at once both superficial and deep. This essay examines how the concept of mutation inspires and stimulates designers to create avant-garde pieces, and how it contributes to the exploration and invention of new materials and production processes. In the conclusion, possible implications of the concept for the future of fashion will be suggested.

Mutation is a theme that many designers and fashion-artists have embraced over the years, not just recently, but also far back in our collective past. For example, making and wearing masks is an ancient form of mutation-through-fashion that persists to this day. From Stone Age tribes to twenty-first century trick-or-treaters, from the Maya in South America to the Dogon in Africa, and from kabuki theater in Japan to masked balls in Venice, masks have been used as a form of disguise and concealment—and transformation—in nearly every era and culture. Masking is perhaps the first or lowest level of fashion mutation, where the change is more symbolic than actual.

Designed to hide the identities of their wearers, masks possess a spiritual power. Their applications range from hunting and warfare to worship and rituals. The use of masks is usually connected to the idea of representing supernatural entities: anthropomorphic ones with human characteristics or theriomorphic ones with animal features. In each case, the wearer mutates into a new type of being.

Exploring the effects of masks, the artist HEYNIEK claims that the most numerous and significant forms and expressions are found in the face. Covering it conveys a stronger message or produces a deeper meaning than camouflaging a different part of the body. Through this symbolic mutation, our imagination is stimulated to enter the unattainable world of the unknown.

Contemporary labels like Maison Margiela and Viktor & Rolf thus began experimenting with this concept of disguise-through-mutation by masking or painting the heads of their models. This approach opened new avenues for many

LUCYANDBART

designers and provided them with an ideal platform to express their vision and artistry without restrictions. Such collections are liberated from the influence of the models' own personalities, meaning that the audience's attention is concentrated solely on the garment. The mask transforms the wearer into something other than, or more than, a mere model.

In addition, our urge to modify or mutate our appearance extends beyond the face and the concept of disguise. The idea of approaching our bodies as a canvas or as a surface to express and reflect our individuality and identity dates back centuries. In fact, the practice of body modification has often been used as an indicator of one's wealth and status. Every culture has its own way of doing so. Circumcision, for instance, has been a private marker of cultural belonging for centuries.

In its more public expressions, this sort of second-level mutation is often associated with the reigning ideals of beauty in each era and region, and thus also comprises a form of fashion. Some have flourished and then died out, like the Chinese practice of binding women's feet to transform them into tiny lotus-shaped appendages. Others have persisted to this day, like the practice of elongating women's necks with ornamental neck rings, which the Kayan, a Tibeto-Burman ethnic minority, have practiced since the eighth century. In the West, figure-shaping, body-morphing corsets were an accepted—and expected—part of women's wardrobes. Interestingly, it is often the female body that is mutated for public display.

In 1997, the Japanese designer Rei Kawakubo pushed the limits of body modification through fashion design by presenting a striking yet provocative collection titled "Dress to Body." The legendary collection, rechristened "lumps and bumps" by the press, approached the female body as a living sculpture, radically changing its silhouette, creating amorphous volumes in unexpected places, and transforming the relationship between the body and that which clothes it.

Others have explored the mutational relationship between the body and what covers it in a different way. For instance, art director and fashion photographer Madame Peripetie approaches her work with an off-kilter aesthetic. Using a variety of materials and props designed and fitted to look like extraterrestrial armor, she does not dress her models' bodies but rather reinvents them. Her audacity and inventiveness results in creatures that are half-human, half-sculpture, wholly abnormal, and yet fully alive.

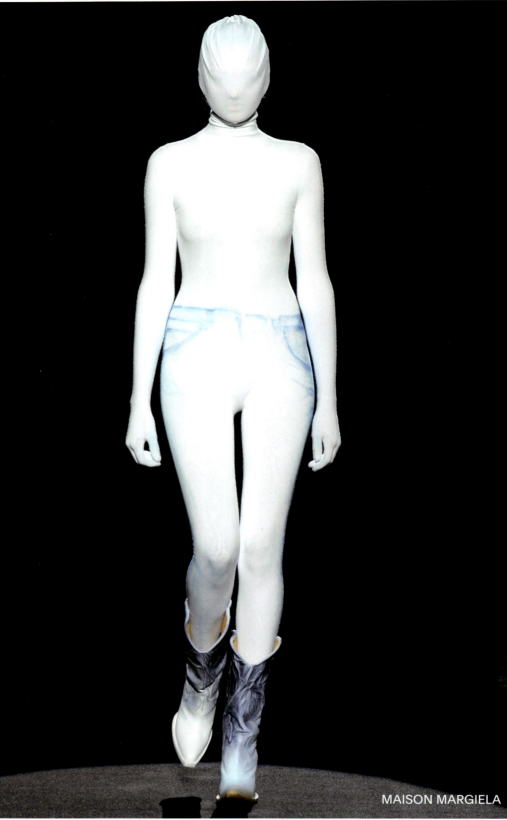

MAISON MARGIELA

From there, the next step seems to be post-humanity. Fascinated by the concept of mutation and what it means for our own future, artist Lucy McRae invents and constructs structures on the skin that reshape the human form. Her "Astronaut Aerobics Institute" project revolves around the idea of the transformation and evolution of the human body and its ability to adapt to space, a wholly new environment that is both hostile to our biology yet rich in potential and symbolism. McRae is fasci-

nated by the concept of survival of the fittest, an idea that indicates the creation of a new breed—a future post-human archetype with a mutated body able to survive in an alternate world.

Whereas McRae's creations seek solutions within the self-imposed limitations of a sort of plausible (though wildly imaginative) fact-based science, the field of character design opens up totally unfettered channels for exploring the mutation of the human body. Intended to shock, to disturb, or to define a new visual language, the concept of mutation questions the established norms of beauty. Ranging from cartoonish to realistic, from genderless to hypersexual, character design in fashion is a hybrid art. These costumes are presented solely in fashion shows, editorial features,

"Through experimentation with a diverse range of mediums and processes, fashion innovators are enveloping the human body in entirely new shapes. For some of them, the goal is not just to mutate the human body, but to mutate matter itself."

"Our wardrobe may one day include futuristic genetic mutations that are echoes of the sort of masks or costumes our ancestors once wore. And by wearing them, we will be touching our future and our past simultaneously."

or museum exhibitions. They are made to be seen, but not to be worn. Their function is not to clothe but to communicate.

However, such communication need not be limited to catwalks and galleries. Lady Gaga has become famous not just for her talent as a musician but also for her bold and often grotesque sense of fashion—a style that often exhibits mutational elements. Her followers have imitated some of her most iconic hair and make-up effects, like the flesh-colored spikes that looked like subdermal implants on her face, which she used during the promotion of her *Born This Way* album. They have also designed their own interpretations of her costumes. By both promoting creativity and pushing the boundaries of what is possible, Lady Gaga has made massive contributions to the fashion world and helped take fashion-mutations off the runway and into real life.

None of these bodily mutations are possible without the use of external materials. Direct genetic mutation is still in the realm of science fiction. However, the interest of artists and designers in creating new forms through mutation has extended into much more complex concepts, such as quantum physics and cosmic consciousness. Through experimentation with a diverse range of mediums and processes, fashion innovators are enveloping the human body in entirely new shapes. For some of them, the goal is not just to mutate the human body, but to mutate matter itself.

The designer Jolan van der Wiel, for instance, concentrates on joining the forces of technology and natural phenomena in an attempt to develop new tools capable of bringing his ideas to life. Material mutation is his means of expression. His projects have resulted in new production processes that allow new forms to take shape.

With "Magnetic Motion," a footwear collaboration with Iris van Herpen, he set out to make his ideas manifest. The textured footwear was created by first mixing iron fillings with resin and then coating a shoe with the magnetic fluid. Van der Wiel then used magnets to create spikes along the surface of the shoes before the material hardened. "Magnetism was one of the most spectacular tools I could create," says van der Wiel. "This force creates form within seconds." The same magnetic mutation technique was used by van der Wiel to develop a hybrid metallo-magnetic fabric for a series of garments for Iris van Herpen's 2013 Paris show. The clothes were not only created through a new process, they themselves were capable of morphing into totally new and unexpected forms as the models walked down the runway.

As futuristic as these projects may seem, the future of mutation in fashion may hold even more in store for us. The artist Bart Hess has speculated that fashion designers will use DNA itself as a design tool, resulting in "cotton that is already designed to grow into a pair of socks … And animals, like a fox in the shape of a coat." Consumers will one day be able to walk into a store and pick a pre-programmed animal form right off the rack.

Our wardrobe may one day include futuristic genetic mutations that are echoes of the sort of masks or costumes our ancestors once wore. And by wearing them, we will be touching our future and our past simultaneously.

JÓLAN VAN DER WIEL

LUCYANDBART

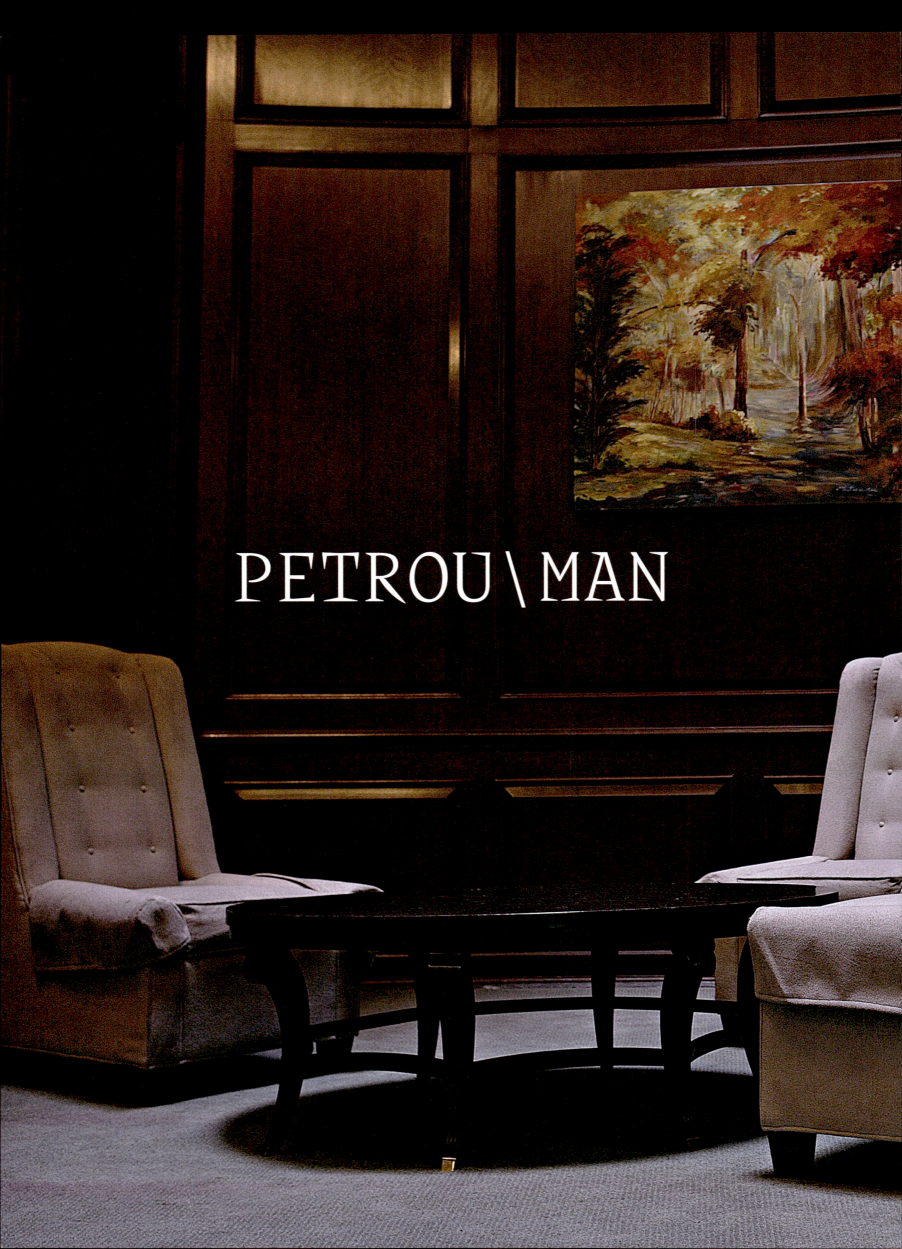

THE FRINGE PROJECTS

VIBSKOV
&
EMENIUS

ALICE
AUAA

LUCY
MCRAE

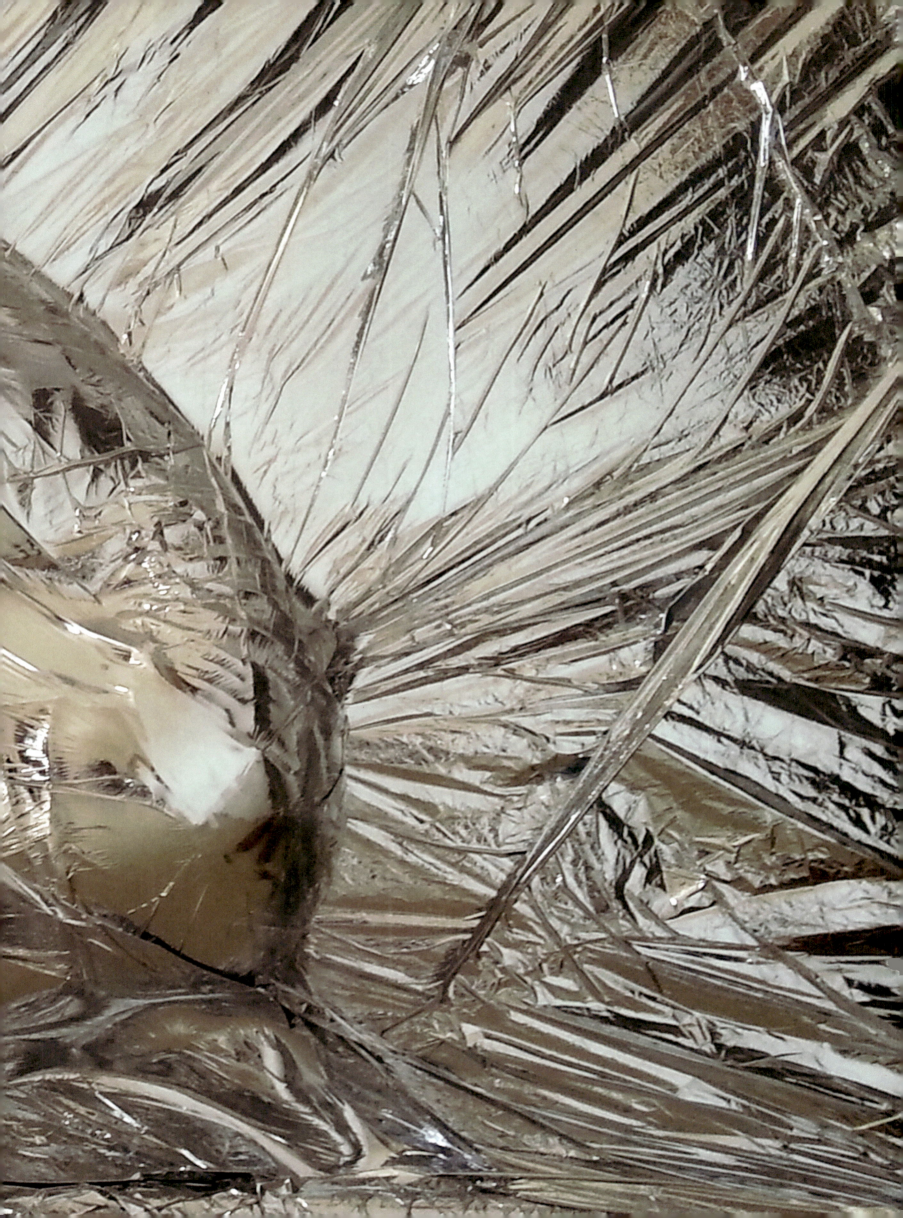

YELLOW SOVEREIGN

KEN
TANABE

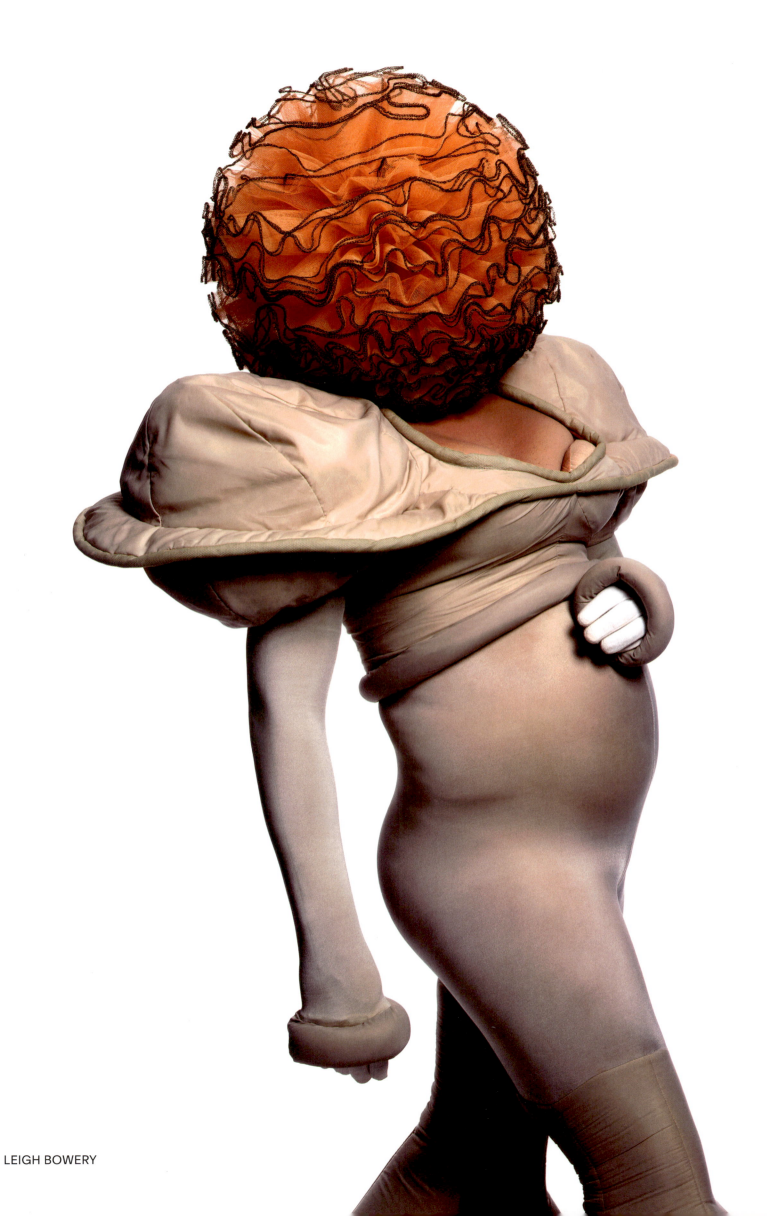

LEIGH BOWERY

MAKING

HOW DESIGNERS SHAPE THE FUTURE AND REMAKE THE PRESENT BY PIONEERING NEW VISIONS, NEW MATERIALS, NEW MEDIA, AND NEW METHODS.

IRIS VAN HERPEN

When we think of the term pioneer, we often picture an explorer breaking new ground, leading the way to undiscovered lands, blazing paths to unseen vistas, and uncovering unimagined possibilities. They are the ones who push forward into the new. They may be adventurers, or scientists, or even artists, but they may equally—if unexpectedly—be fashion designers. But what distinguishes pioneers in the world of fashion, particularly in the context of the otherworldly, is not just the media with which they work, but also the fact that they so often reject the hunt for a solution, and so frequently set out to ask a question in the first place.

The system of fashion is based on a condition of constant renewal. Within the fashion design cycle, with its biannual seasons, there is never a full stop. The book is never closed; no final answer is ever given. This constant thirst for newness means that the role of the designer is never complete. The perpetual nature of innovation means they are constantly searching for different ways of creating clothes and staging new ideas. It has led to the fall of many great designers from renowned fashion houses. However, this quick cycle also allows us to easily single out those that have truly acquired the status of pioneers by challenging the very fabric of our cultural landscape.

Thierry Mugler was one such designer. The codes of 1980s fashion had become dated and the scene was a caricature of itself: neon ravers, sports tracksuits, and a whole lot of hair. Yet Mugler was able to enact a total rejection of the prevailing trends. He loathed the world around him and dreamed of creating another. And he did just that, integrating technology, architecture, science, and fashion with an aim to provide not comfort but confidence to those who donned his designs. He presented a radicalized projection of womanhood—one that completely shunned the classical approach to femininity. Mugler's women were superheroines and sirens who did not slink, but rather

THE NEXT
WORLD by
GREG FRENCH

strutted along the streets. It was to be the birth of a new way of power dressing, one that scrutinized the lines of the body, accentuating them as part of a dramatic spectacle. "The potential of your body," as Mugler once said, "is endless."

Confidence is an important tool within pioneering fashion. The transformative power of clothing is of crucial importance, an issue that relates back to our earlier exploration of fashion's obsession with the new. The new can equip us with a sense of differentiation and excitement, breaking us out of the conventions of the everyday. No man ever epitomized this better than London-based creative Leigh Bowery, whose skewed vision of commonplace dress was born out of a lifestyle that rejected the mundane and embraced the vivacity of the capital's club scene.

That club scene was to act as a laboratory for the radical creations of fashion's vanguard. There was a sense of the otherworldly in walking into one of Bowery's club nights, which attendees declared were "lands of deranged, decadent expression." Soho was Bowery's petri dish; his outlandish outfits and performances were his experimental catalysts. Leigh adopted masks to hide the human face, used ribbon bindings to conceal the wearer's genitals and turn them into a genderless being, and employed PVC as an adornment for his new breed of poly-sexual aliens. It was shocking enough to grab the headlines of the daily papers and draw creatives from around the world to London. The result was a collision of fashion, dance, music, and performance that spawned new ideas behind closed

doors and introduced them to the outside world. Bowery's dress signified a shift toward individualism and an attitude where there was only ever a wrong way of dressing. Originality was power in the eclectic, frenetic, ever-changing club scene.

If transformation and originality are the traits inherent to a pioneer, then Lee Alexander McQueen was to take those attributes to a whole new level. The so-called *enfant terrible* of British fashion, McQueen was certainly influenced by Bowery's Soho. Yet rather than turning back to club culture, he looked to the fragility, beauty, and might of nature to inform his designs. While other designers presented dull collections on plain white catwalks, McQueen fearlessly played out the fantastical stories of his mind, redefining what a fashion show could be. And fearlessness breeds innovation, as it did in McQueen's final show, Plato's Atlantis. The show itself was to push technology to its limit, not only in the way it was staged, but also in the way it was presented. For the first time, fashion was streamed live over the internet, making fashion accessible to the masses and encouraging active engagement with it. No longer was the runway event reserved exclusively for the privileged ticket holder; instead, it became available to anyone who chose to tune in. Fashion was no longer a sealed world—its audience was invited to embrace it for all its eccentricities.

It is thanks to the likes of McQueen that the internet has become a meeting place for revolutionary designers who are no longer confined to gritty underground clubs or overpriced art institutions. Facilitating an easy exchange of ideas, the digital is a language that pioneers have become fluent in. Under creative director Shayne Oliver, New York label Hood By Air has recognized its effectiveness, creating a network of worldwide contributors who have helped to define the groundbreaking new label. Hood By Air brings together elements of design, performance, gender ambiguity, subculture, and technology. Gender identities have become fertile subject matter as these five attributes subvert dress for the twenty-first century. There is an element of deconstruction in nearly everything that the label does. Slashes, open zippers, and frayed edges are presented with de-sexualized styling that includes hair extensions, color contact lenses, and shaved hair. Yet the result is by no means a costume. Instead Oliver presents an array of gender codes that have been re-hashed in light of the modern day consumer. The fashions speak volumes about the wider socio-political changes in New York City. They reflect an acceptance of new gender and racial identities, a development that is demonstrated through a mutation of fashion that no longer hides behind masks or costumes, but instead has a distinctiveness all on its own.

THIERRY MUGLER

ALEXANDER McQUEEN

On this note of destruction, let us return to that initial thought about the fashion system and its state of constant reinvention, about how the role of the designer is never quite complete. This incompleteness is the reason why we have seen the likes of Kawakubo or Karl Lagerfeld remain for some thirty years at the head of the houses of Comme des Garçons and Chanel, respectively. Every season represents the start of a brand new path or story. There are thus continued attempts to be rebellious or modern, or even attempts to pioneer from *within* the fashion system, but sometimes it takes a true pioneer to show us a route away from the runway, a path truly removed from traditional notions of how things are done.

It is in this spirit that Iris van Herpen exploits the twenty-first century for its revolutionary technologies, and she continues to push the capabilities of artificial intelligence through 3D printing and alternative materials. In doing so, she has turned concepts of fashion creation on their head and raised some interesting questions that may change the way designers work. If a computer has the ability to construct a garment itself, does the role of the designer become obsolete? Is human craftsmanship in jeopardy? For van Herpen, the answer in each case is no—not because she wishes to cling to the past, but because she is so open to the future. Machinery may cut down the time required to produce a particular garment by removing human labor from the equation—yet it also cuts designers free from temporal restraints, allowing them to execute more ambitious visions. Her machines need her curating eye and technical hand as much as she needs her machines to help produce her pioneering designs. Out of this collaborative friction come garments that would once have been considered impossible.

Fashion itself is a gigantic mutant beast, changing its face and form every day to reflect and provoke those who help feed it. While the designers who do this may work in opposing ways, their shared goal of presenting something new is what defines them as pioneers. To achieve that goal, they must be true masters of subversion—stepping defiantly beyond or even against the zeitgeist in order to constantly redefine it. That liminal space is where the differentiation of the fashion pioneer lies. No sooner do we think we have found an answer to the questions they have raised than another has been posed. They move fashion forward as though feeding coal into a gigantic locomotive on a never-ending track. Without the determination to present something new, that train would grind to a halt. As Rei Kawakubo said, "Creation takes things forward. Without anything new there is no progress. Creation equals new." True pioneers can and must rise to that challenge. And that is why the future of fashion is very exciting indeed.

"Fashion is a beast that changes its face and form every day to reflect and provoke those who feed it. While designers may work in opposing ways, their shared goal of presenting something new is what defines them as pioneers. To achieve that goal, they must be true masters of subversion."

Hood By Air's approach may be new, but they are not the only designers to make pioneering attempts to use fashion to redefine how we perceive gender. Japanese designer Rei Kawakubo, the creative director of Comme des Garçons ("like a boy"), creates garments that actively challenge the idea of masculine and feminine, but not through the predictable inclusion of skirts, shirts, and dresses. Far more radical are Kawakubo's silhouettes, which are not designed to be sexual, but rather to provide a deeper sense of satisfaction to the wearer. Swathes of fabric, two-dimensional silhouettes, and impossible geometric shapes transform the body from recognizable anthropoid to walking work of art. Her vision is just as unapologetically ruthless today as it was at her 1981 debut when a shocked audience nicknamed her baffling creations "Hiroshima's revenge" in reaction to the radical shapes and volumes of fabric she employed.

JAMES
T MERRY

MOTH AND VOCAL CHORD MASK

HIDEKI SEO

NIGHT BLOOMONG CEREUS

HEART

PRAY

FLOW

STATE OF FLUX

by

IDA GRO CHRISTIANSEN

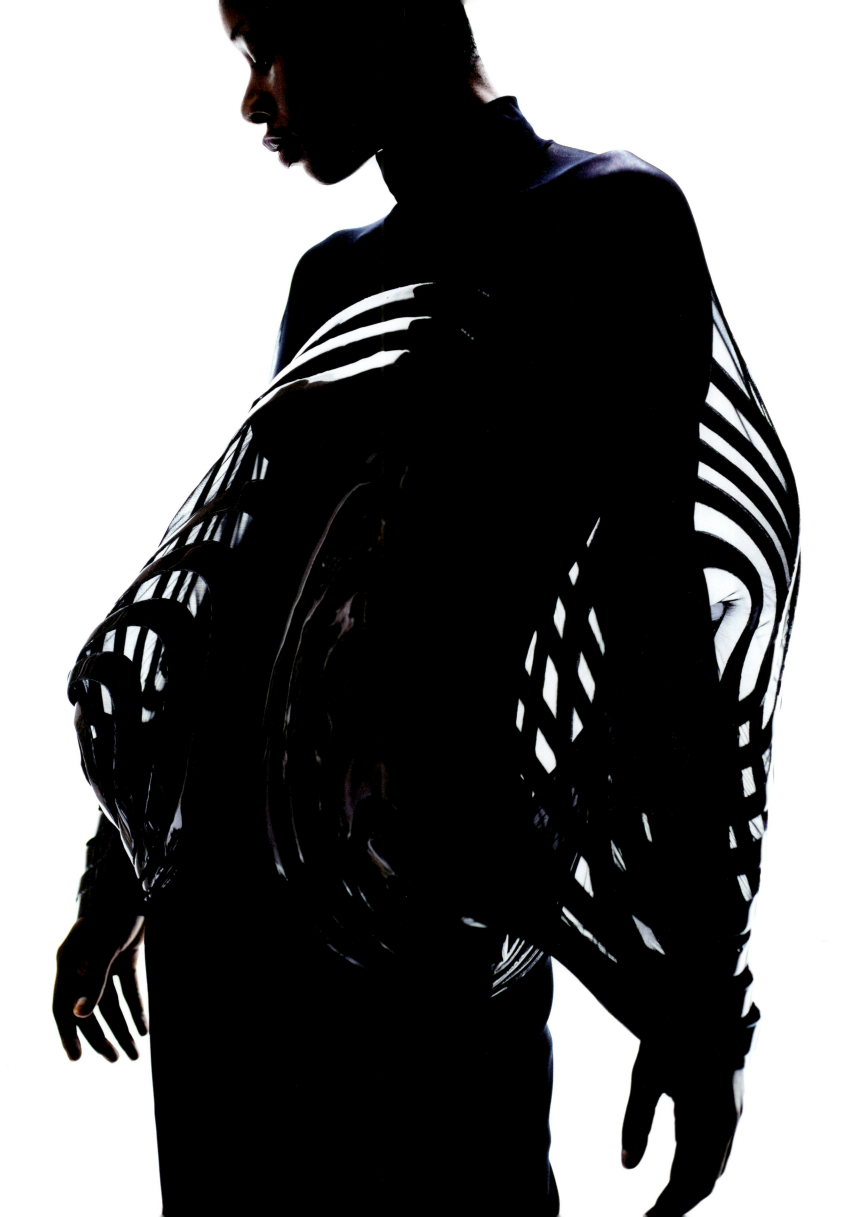

TANEL VEENRE

DZHUS

TECHNOGENESIS

TOTALITARIUM

TOTALITARIUM

ARCHETYPE

BURNT

by

ROBERT WUN

KATIE
ROBERTS
WOOD

SYNCH

SUPER SONIC BOOM

THE
ANOMALIES

JOJO ROSS

DISTORTED THINKING
PATTERN

TEN OUT OF TEN

RENEE NICOLE SANDER

DE.FI.CIENCY

ROBERT
WUN
VOLT

ALEXANDER MCQUEEN

PORTRAIT

The work of LEE ALEXANDER MCQUEEN**, born in London in 1969,
is perhaps one of the most documented and talked about oeuvres in the world.
With its autobiographical approach to fashion, Lee's work was about the way
he lived his own life and the darker aspects of the human psyche that he
himself experienced.**

Beginning with "Jack the Ripper Stalks His Victims," his 1992 Central Saint Martins graduation collection, a heightened level of storytelling would be inherent in all of his designs. Fantasy was a key aspect of everything he did, from his spectacular runway shows, which were produced in part with the production company Gainsbury & Whiting, to the imagery he created with some of the industry's most revered photographers. McQueen conjured worlds in which the pains of reality could be both escaped and explored in equal measure.

Early in his career, McQueen trained with Savile Row tailors Gieves & Hawkes. It was there that he began to develop his crucial understanding—and love—of the human body, which went on to inform every aspect of his design process. This can be seen in the vast amount of iconic pieces in his renowned body of work, including the notorious bumsters, which were pants cut so that the top of the rear was left exposed. His grasp of the female form and his exploration of its most integral details gave his customers the ability to enter an entirely different world simply by putting on McQueen's clothing. Wearing his clothes was a transformative experience. "I took it to the extreme," he once said. "The girls looked menacing, because there was so much top and so little bottom, because of the length of the legs."

2015 saw Lee's work take center stage at the Victoria and Albert Museum's "Savage Beauty" exhibition. The show, part of which was previously staged at the Metropolitan Museum of Art, took visitors through the impossibly wondrous mind of McQueen, from his controversial "Highland Rape" collection to the futuristic vision of humanity that played out in his final show, "Plato's Atlantis." His productive collaborations with milliner Philip Treacy and jeweler Shaun Leane, and his friendship with Isabella Blow—all figures who were paramount in fostering McQueen's ability to radically change the appearance of the human body—were also explored.

McQueen was perhaps best known for his lavish productions, which conjured up dream worlds in which the characters he created were revealed to shocked editors aghast at the brutality and darkness that underpinned his work. Over time, however, they gradually fell in love with his creations, like models trapped in a one-way mirrored box or the specter-like appearance of a hologram of Kate Moss.

If there was a single thread that ran through all the work he produced, it was his constant thirst for exploring the issues that we as humans face in our day-to-day lives. Fashion granted him the ability to express the self, to present the workings of the mind, and, ultimately, to change our perception of the world in which we live.

ALEXANDER MCQUEEN: SAVAGE BEAUTY AT THE V&A

ALEX
ULICHNY

MARKO
MITANOVSKI

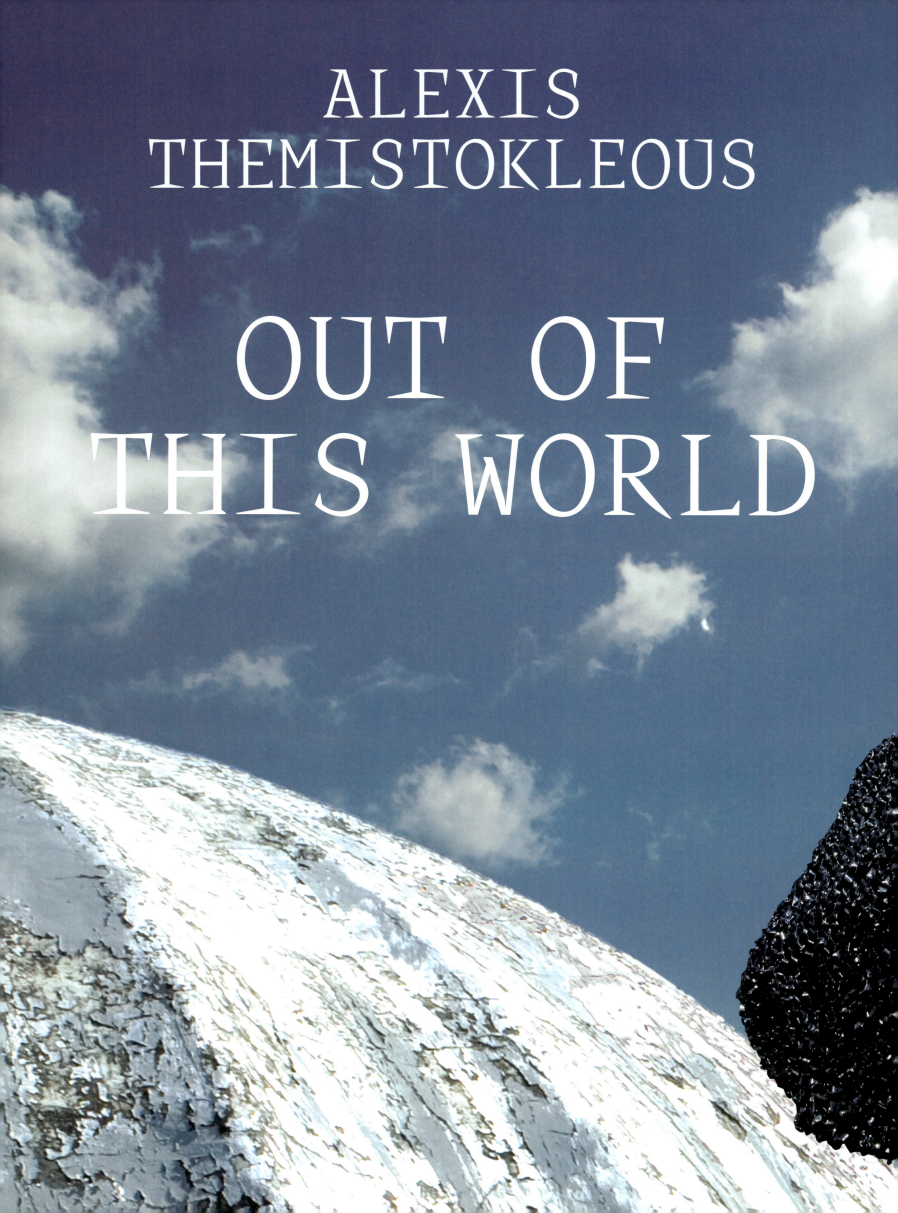

ALEXIS THEMISTOKLEOUS

OUT OF THIS WORLD

PETER MOVRIN

00.00

KONSTANTIN KOFTA

ORB

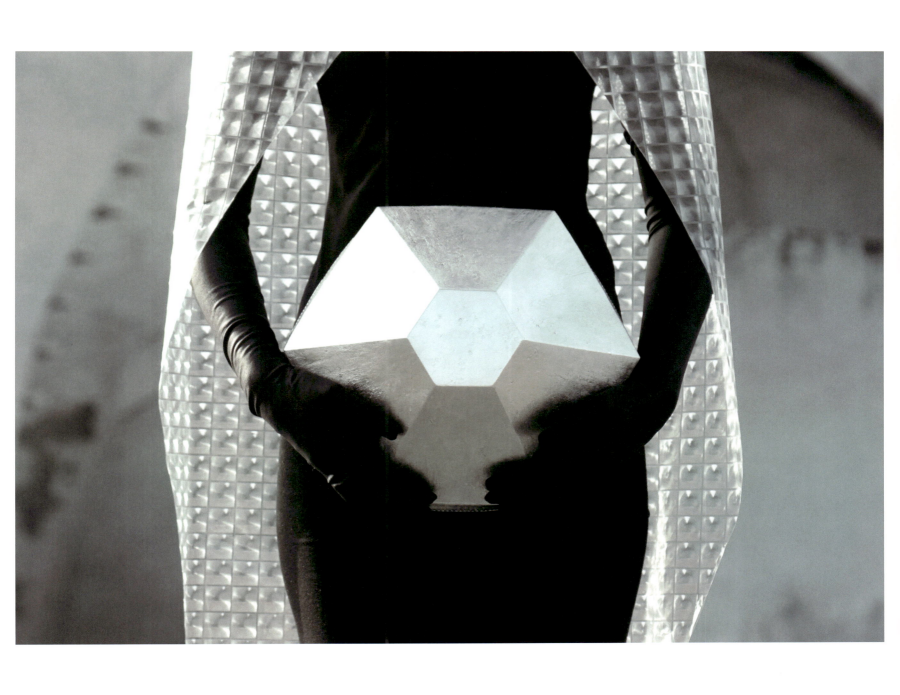

INERTIA

JAZZ KUIPERS

HAVOC

DYL

X-TREME
CONQUISTADORS

THEO-MASS
LEXILEICTOUS

EXTRATERRESTRIAL

THE MUTANTS RETURN

PACO PEREGRÍN

PORTRAIT

Spanish-born PACO PEREGRÍN **is an image-maker whose work questions
society's preconceptions of identity and beauty. There is a sense of
theatricality to his work, which fuses vibrant makeup and dramatic lighting
with inspired styling in order to transform the human body from a mundane
object into an enigmatic spectacle.**

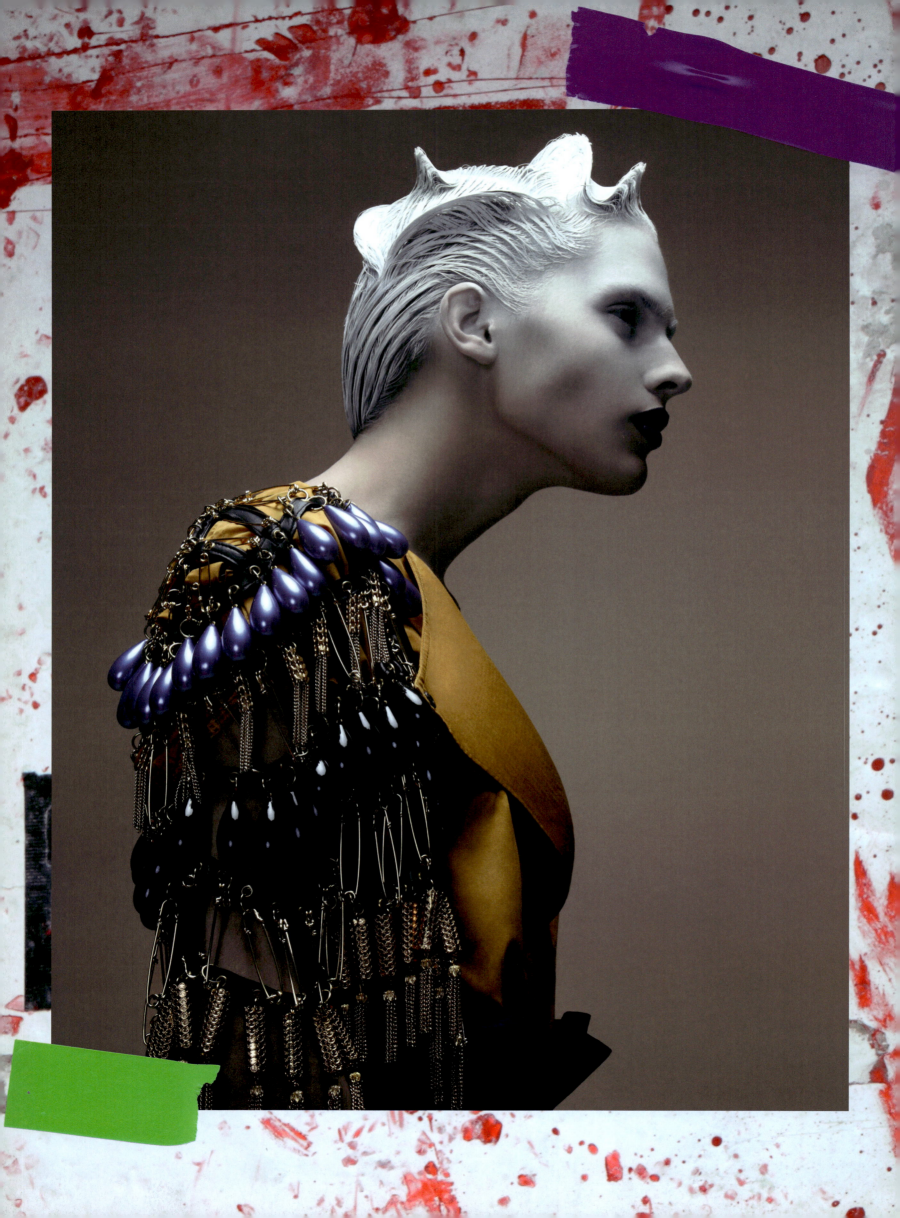

Peregrín studied fine art at the University of Seville and developed an interest in the fields of design, painting, and theater—disciplines that have had a clear impact on his approach to fashion photography. It was within the construction of the fashion image that he would combine his love of those art forms and create a means of expressing his innermost thoughts. As a result, his work has gained international recognition, and has been shown on the gallery walls of some of the world's leading institutions and featured on the pages of leading fashion magazines like *Vogue, Elle,* and *Vanity Fair.*

His models are often shot against stark white or gray backgrounds—an illusionary technique that forces the eye to focus solely on the mesmerizing characters that live within his imagery. The skin is used as a canvas—a place to explore a sense of inner beauty, hinting at something that the eye itself cannot see. Bright splashes of acidic color sit alongside bespoke pieces of costume, conjuring mystical beings.

This approach is shown most clearly in a recent body of work entitled *Facing,* produced in part for the Marie Dalgar Crossover Art Project in China. Presented as part of the project's runway show, a gigantic white sculpted face hung above the audience; over time, the face was transformed by color and light as Peregrín's projections danced across the 3D form. The work questioned notions of physiognomy and our classical understanding of poise and beauty while also showing how contemporary fashion and makeup has provided us with the opportunity and means to radically change our image.

Peregrín's work exudes a sense of uneasiness as it explores these metamorphic notions, a feeling that is mostly due to the otherworldly alterations that are so vital to his work. Part human, part extraterrestrial life-form, Peregrín creates dark images in which the boundaries between reality and fantasy are blurred. It is through this collision in his photography that we are encouraged to turn the mirror back upon ourselves, explore our own perceptions of beauty, and better our understanding of the world around us.

The merging of various art forms makes Peregrín's images particularly identifiable. His photography resides somewhere between commercial asset and work of art, a crossover that enables him to explore characteristic traits and their applications within the market. For Peregrín, fashion presents us with a rare ability to completely transform ourselves into something or someone else, a stance that remains at the core of his artistic practice.

ALIEN BEAUTIES

by

PACO PEREGRÍN

NOBLEZA
FUTURISTA

NONSENSE
IN THE DARK

BEAUTIFUL
MONSTER

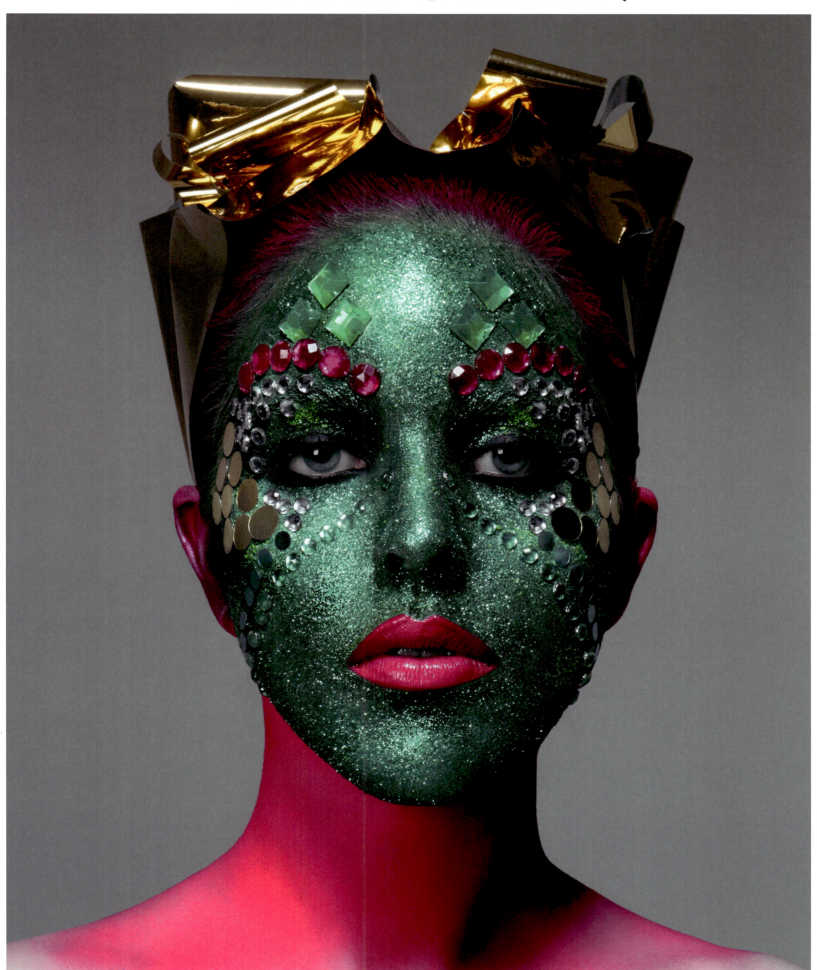

JEAN PAUL GAULTIER

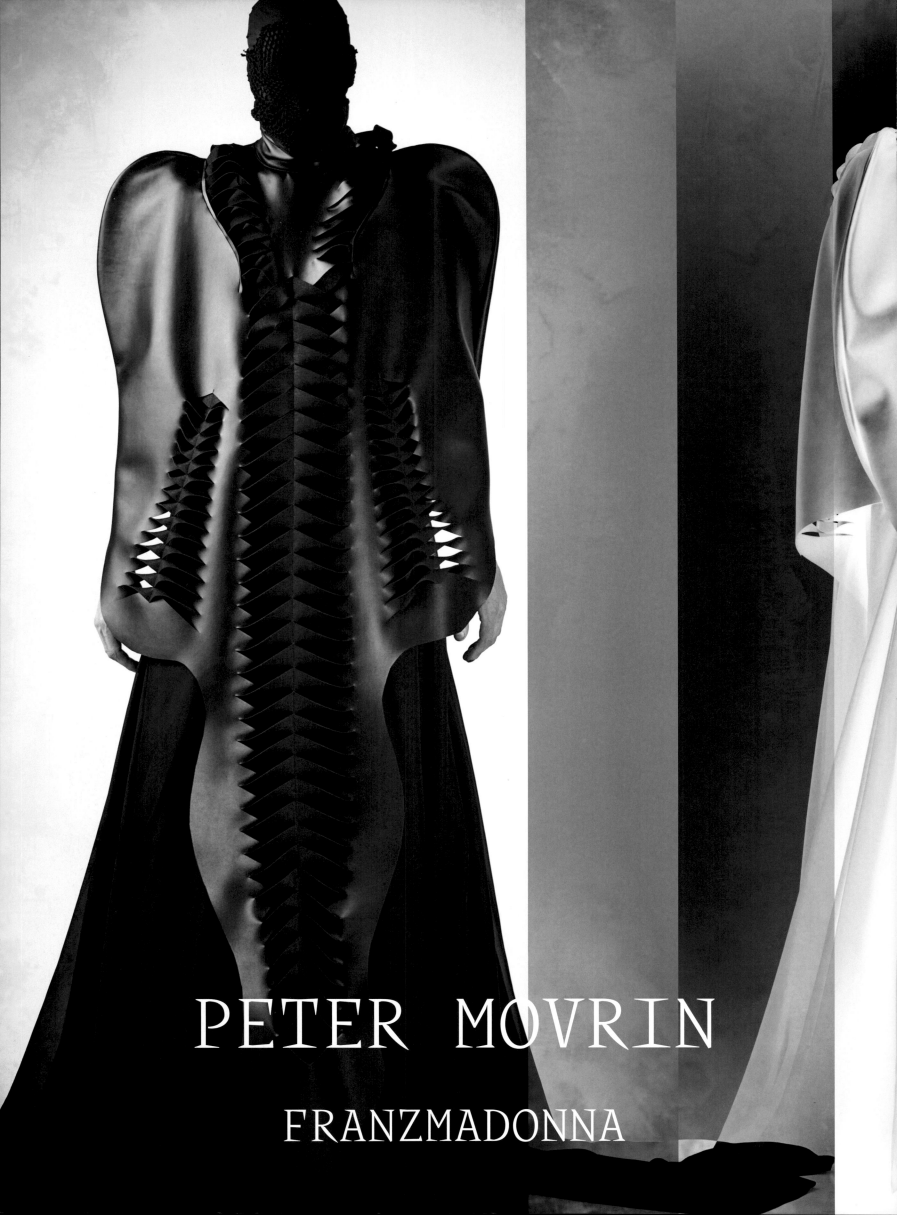

PETER MOVRIN

FRANZMADONNA

DANIEL SANNWALD

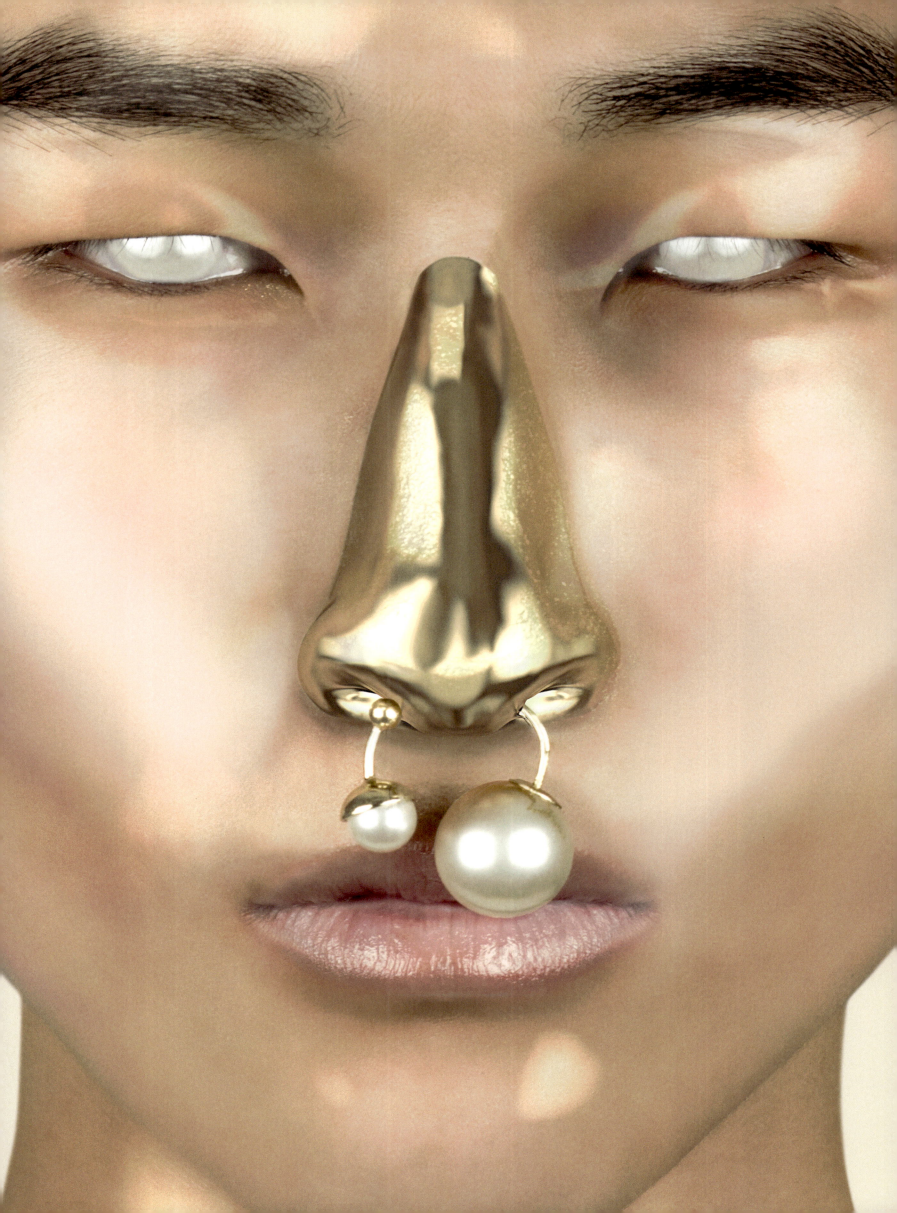

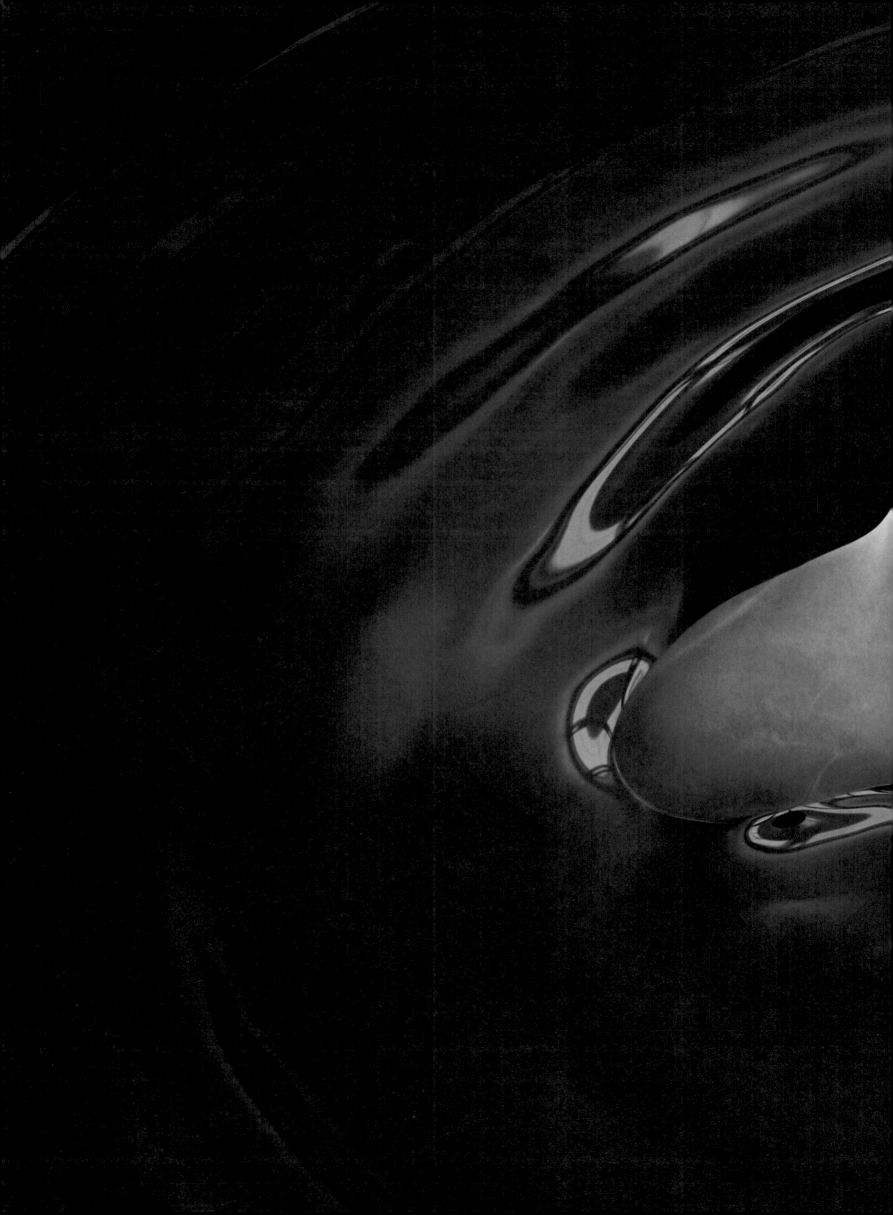

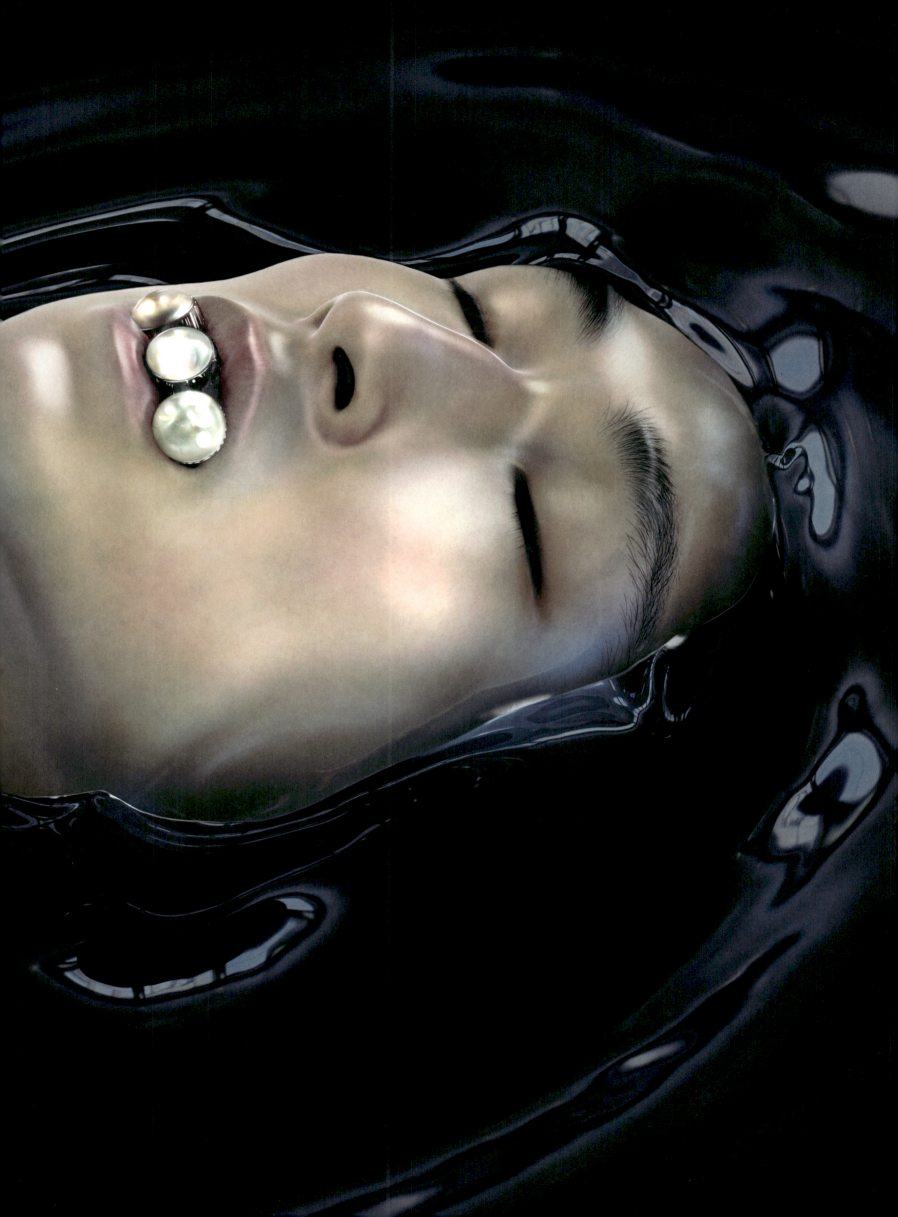

EDMUND
001

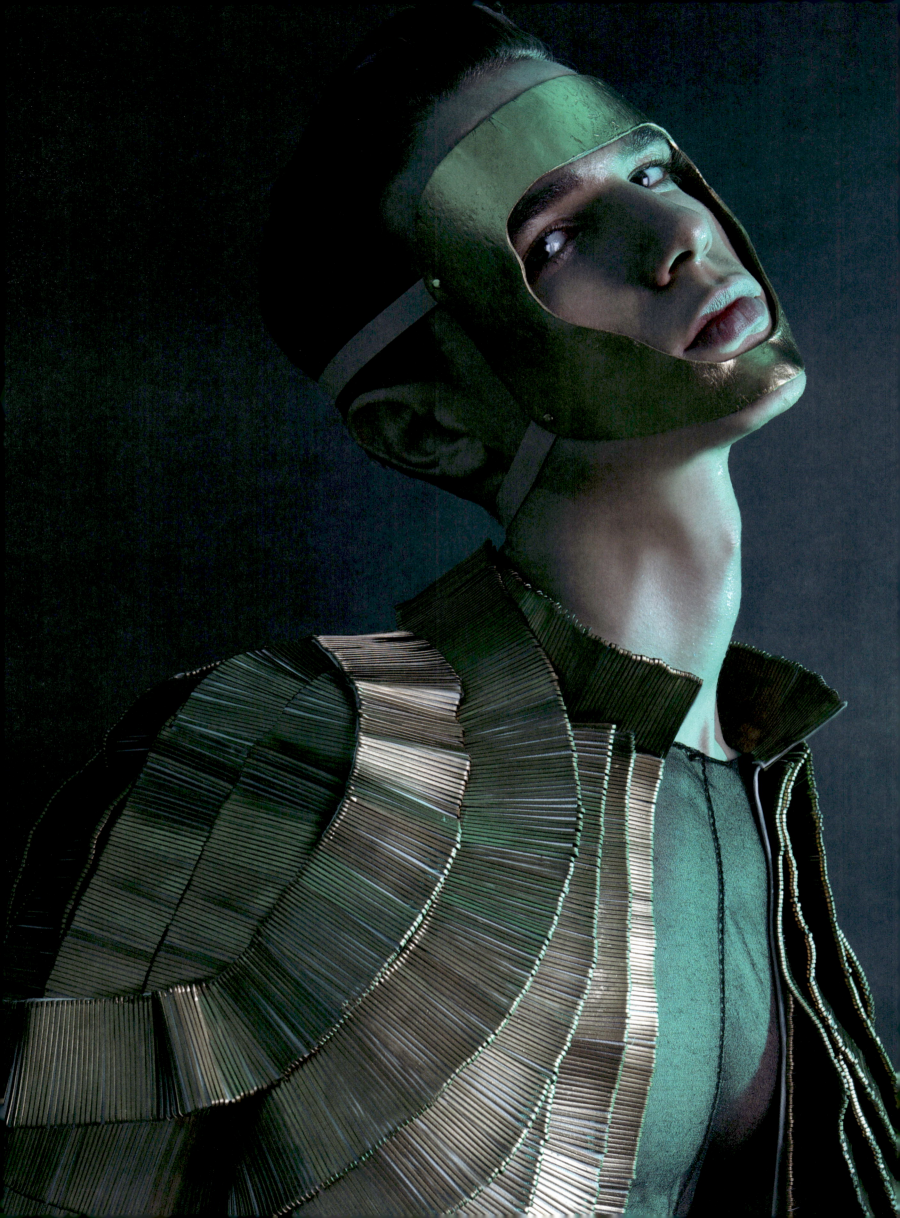

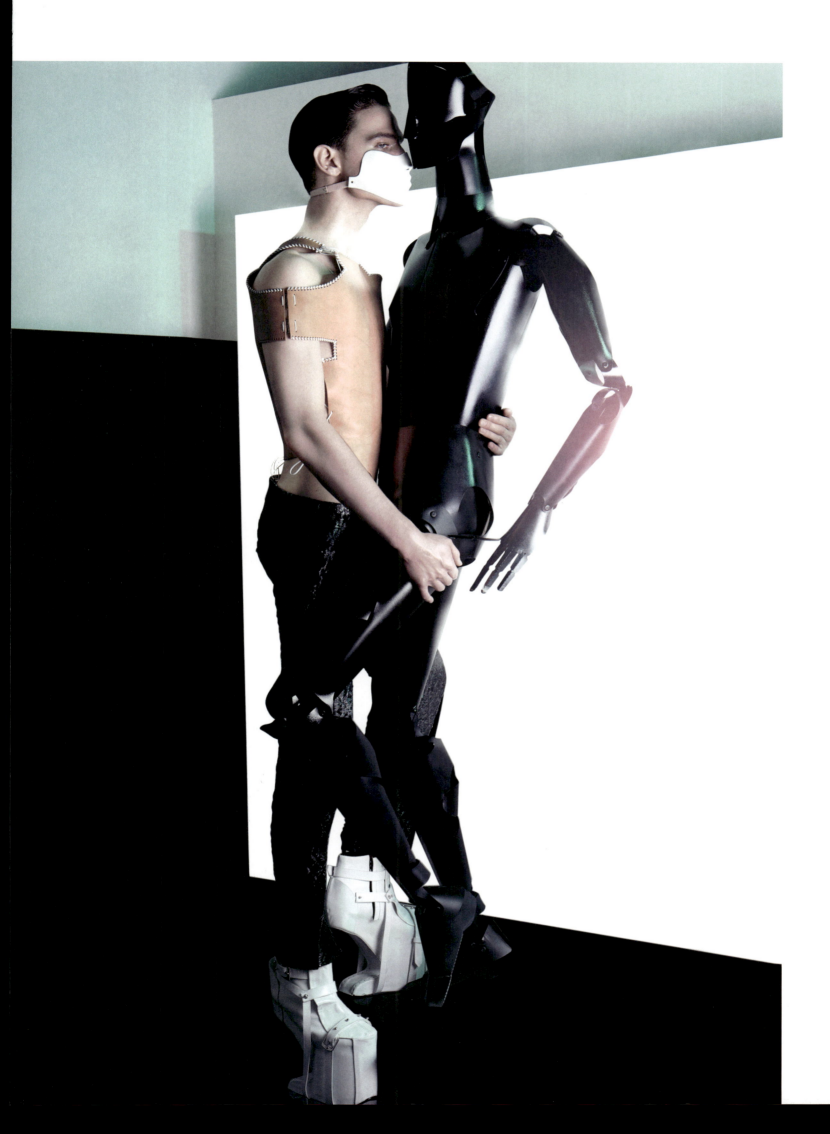

NIXI KILLICK

FUTURE-TIVE
NATURE

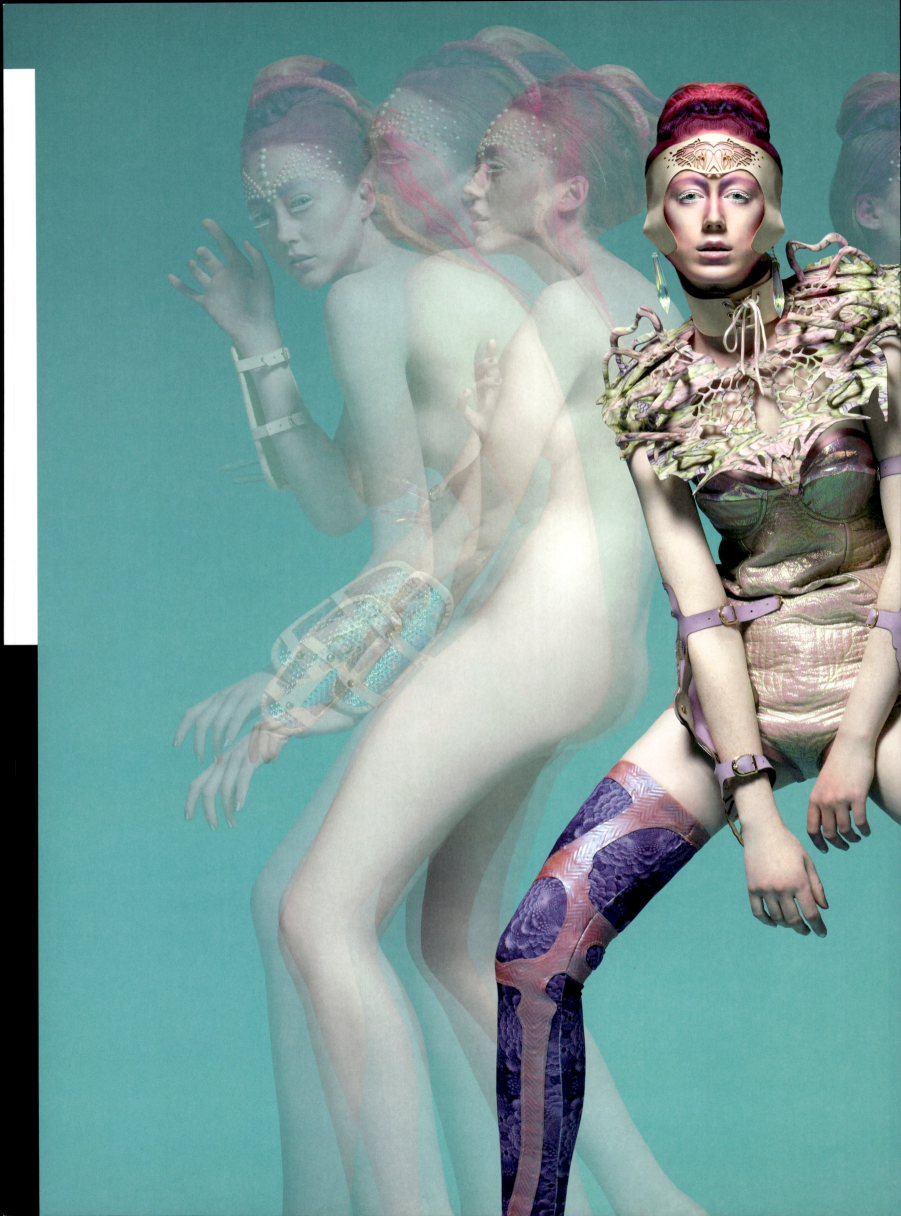

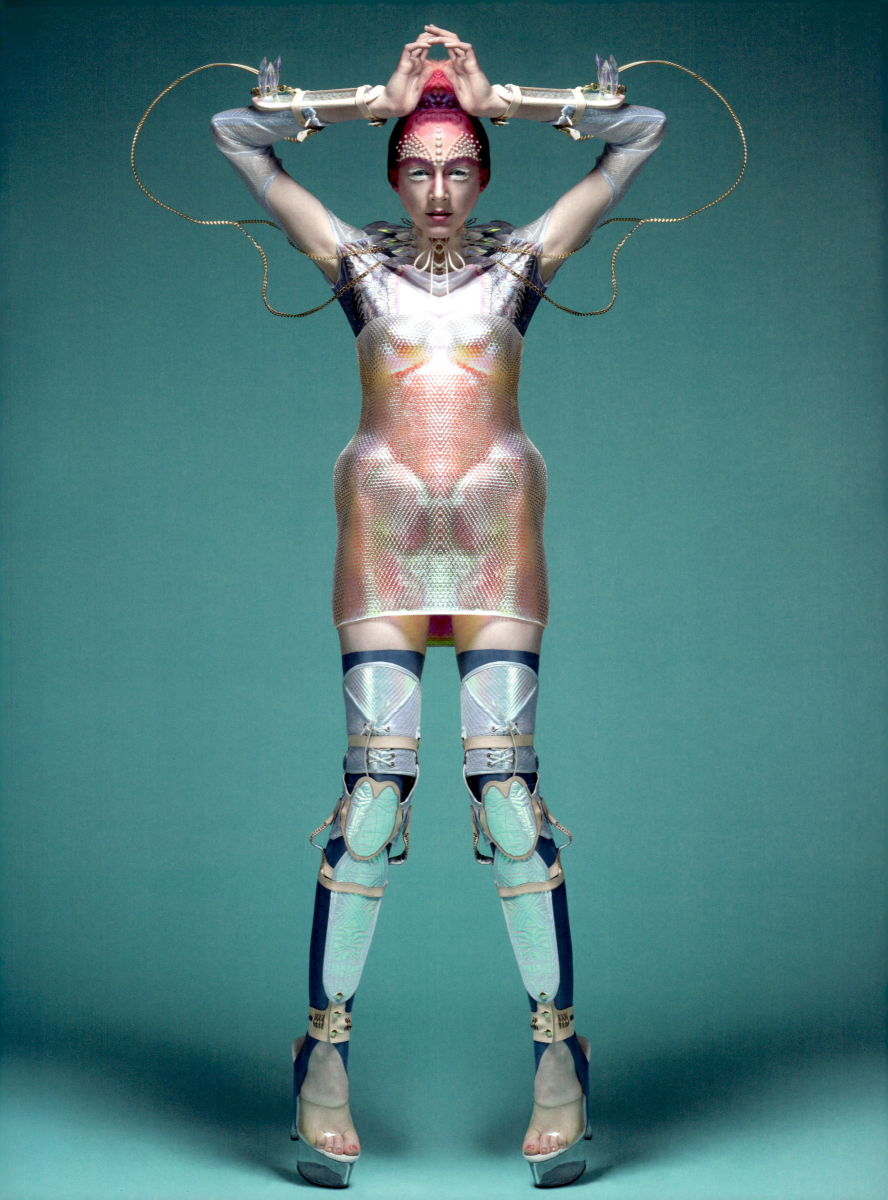

PHILIPS x STUDIO XO

HAUTE

HOW DESIGNERS ARE USING TECHNOLOGY TO FASHION A FUTURE OF ADAPTIVE FABRICS, MECHANIZED MATERIALS, INTERACTIVE OUTFITS, AND PUSH-BUTTON COUTURE.

Technology is creating new ways to do and make and even dream, ushering in a whole new era for the fashion world. Designs that in the past would have been difficult to imagine, let alone realize, are now just a click away from production. And the choices, not only of materials themselves but also of the ways they can be used and combined, are infinite. Fabric gives way to titanium; sewing yields to 3D printing. Stainless steel armor, super-shiny respirators, carbon fiber boots, 3D-printed glasses, and robotic costumes are only a few examples of what can now be achieved.

And yet, even though the range of high-tech design methods is expanding and the use of technology is becoming more prevalent, designers have not always been able to see the true potential available to them. Technological advances have clearly influenced a number of designers in the past—the evidence is there in their collections and fashion shows. In the early years, though, these designers used technology principally as a means of creating spectacular effects on the runway rather than applying it to the garments themselves. Technology was initially used merely to put on a show, and then it became an integral part of the show, and it is only now that we are finally seeing it used to make an impact in the real world.

For instance, Alexander McQueen is lauded as a visionary designer, yet his foray into technology for his spring 1999 show only used technology as a prop. Models strutted past robots onstage, but the sole interplay between tech and fashion occurred when two of the bots spray-painted the model Shalom Harlow as she stood on a rotating platform. As impressive as it may have been as a fashion show, is was only a superficial example of technology interacting with fashion.

Three years later, a show by Viktor & Rolf would attempt to actually blend technology and fashion together—though still in the context of runway showmanship. They created a collection using blue chroma key fabric. This material is not typically used for clothing. Its origins are actually in the movie industry, where it is used as a background onto which all kinds of images can be projected. For the show, two massive screens of the same material were placed behind the catwalk whilst videos of nature and cityscapes were projected onto the background and the models' outfits simultaneously. The result: the models' bodies, and their clothes, continually disappeared, becoming one with the larger images. The designers' goal was to demonstrate Yves Klein's exclamation "Long live the immaterial!"—and technology was the means to that end.

Neither McQueen nor Viktor & Rolf were concerned with the creation of actual wearable technology. Their interest instead was two-fold: one, how the question of technology could create an attention-grabbing interpretation of their vision, and two, how it could subsequently be used to stage a spectacular catwalk show for their audience. Still, it was only a matter of time before designers would adopt technological innovations for use in their own wearable designs.

HUSSEIN CHALAYAN

by THEO-MASS LEXILEICTOUS

TECH-NOLOGIE

Hussein Chalayan was one of the first to do so, experimenting with wearable technology in complex shapes and forms. Chalayan's work focuses on more than just functionality—it also pushes boundaries and challenges preconceived notions related to the general definition of clothing. And while McQueen and Viktor & Rolf merely used robotics and lighting effects to stage their shows, Chalayan actually used these same technologies as integral parts of his garments. Fashion design, its presentation, and its physical realization are becoming inseparable from technology.

For instance, for Chalayan's "Morphing Dress" collection, he integrated microcontrollers into a series of garments that transformed as the models walked down the runway: their dresses rose, shrank, shifted, and changed color. The first model appeared onstage wearing what seemed to be a costume from 1906. As she walked down the catwalk, it progressively transformed into a design from 1916, and then into one from 1926. In the end, the model finished her walk wearing a beaded flapper dress, a radical departure from the original garment. The next two dresses underwent similar time-travelling transformations. In the past, such transformations would have been achieved by simply removing or manipulating pieces of the garments in the course of the walk. Now, however, it is possible for garments to change on their own.

Chalayan has not been alone in exploring and pushing the boundaries of wearable technology. More recently, Beijing-based fashion designer Vega Zaishi Wang created a collection using electroluminescent fabric. Deriving her inspiration from the universe, her "Alpha Lyrae" special collection was a visual spectacle that transcended traditional approaches to realizing fashion designs. "I originally wanted to print patterns of the nebula directly onto the fabric, but then I realized that the best way to combine light and cloth was to use a material with a clean white surface and to combine that with electroluminescent material that has a futuristic blue glow on it," said Wang. Each of these futuristic, structural pieces has a digital controller that streams spaced-out animations across the material.

While Chalayan's and Wang's collections are clear examples of technology and fashion interacting to create something new, they are still confined to the runway. A bridge needs to be built between high fashion and everyday life—and, as they have in the past, it is pop stars

FRANCIS BITONTI STUDIO x MICHAEL SCHMIDT

who are acting as intermediaries by commissioning and wearing tech-couture for their performances and appearances.

New designers are rising to meet these new needs. Studio XO is a London-based fashion/technology company operating at the intersection of science, technology, fashion, and music. They have created pieces for a number of pop stars and celebrities, mainly for their performances, and have developed advanced technologies to be applied to each of their creations. Their creations include a flying hovercraft-dress for Lady Gaga, a digital mermaid bra designed for Azealia Banks, which features crystals that sparkle in real-time to match the rhythm of her rapping, and Bubelle, a dress that senses

the wearer's mood and changes color to match. Studio XO's couture technologies place special emphasis on the body in the twenty-first century.

Technology has thus made an impact on the runway and on pop culture, helping to spread new concepts and approaches, but the long-term effects of technology on fashion are still unclear. High tech fabrics, robotics, and kinetic dresses on the catwalk or in music videos have allowed technology and fashion to co-exist in a kind of equilibrium. On the other hand, due to the rapid development of technology, many believe that advances in industrial production will result in the extinction of the kind of craftsmanship that currently distinguishes fashion. There is a fear that artisanal techniques known only to a few individuals may soon become extinct as more young people choose to dedicate their careers to exploring new technologies.

Addressing that concern, Michael Schmidt's 3D-printed dress for burlesque dancer Dita von Teese is a wear-

> "Thier work focuses on more than just functionality—it also pushes boundaries and challenges preconceived notions related to the general definition of clothing. Fashion design, its presentation, and its physical realization are becoming inseparable from technology."

"In this new and complex era defined by perpetual change, fashion moves forward, reinventing and revolutionizing the human body. An intimate interaction between robotics, craftsmanship, and the human touch will soon be within our grasp."

able masterpiece that merges technology with craftsmanship. Produced to match von Teese's measurements exactly, the dress consists of several pieces assembled with thousands of joints, allowing the dress to follow the movement of her body. Covered in thousands of Swarovski crystals, the black dress is a declaration that nothing would be possible without the element of human intervention. And yet, although a great deal of the work was done by hand, it can also be said that the designer's approach resembles that of an architect wielding powerful software.

This use of technology to create the look of a garment and actually produce it was both inspired and inspiring, but also very much a one-of-a-kind event. What about equally intricate, beautiful, and inspiring practical uses? Today, 3D printing is predominantly used by many designers and artists as a production process; it would thus be quite interesting to explore what a Parisian house would do with it. Luxury brand customers are fascinated by the concept of made-to-order garments and the unimaginable time and expense required to produce a handmade leather handbag or piece of jewelry. But what happens in the event one of those

brands begins producing its goods with a 3D printer?

Karl Lagerfeld has been experimenting with 3D printing for some time now. At Chanel's fall 2015 haute couture show, some of the brand's popular tweed pieces were created using a 3D printer. With brands like Chanel supporting such technologies, it will be extremely interesting to see what luxury brands in general do in response. The result may be a whole new conception of how one perceives and comprehends luxury.

By 3D-printing Chanel's iconic jacket, Lagerfeld used technology to transform a twentieth century signature piece into a twenty-first century statement: fashion moves forward. Since the fashion industry is continuously changing, evolving, and adapting to its environment, one can expect that 3D printing and other new technologies will eventually be embraced by such iconic brands.

As abstract as it may have sounded in the past, the rapid development of technology will soon promote autonomy, offering us the possibility to design and 3D-print our own personalized accessories and clothes at home. Designers will soon be selling ready-to-print blueprints directly

to the user. And while 3D printing has not yet entered the average home, it is certainly on its way to affordability.

Just as industrialization and modernization once blurred the line between handcrafted and machine-made products, technology is sure to hold even more in store for fashion in the very near future. Although the future of the fashion industry remains hard to predict, we can undoubtedly say that its complexity will increase. In this new and complex era defined by perpetual change, fashion moves forward, reinventing and revolutionizing the human body. An intimate interaction between robotics, craftsmanship, and the human touch will soon be within our grasp.

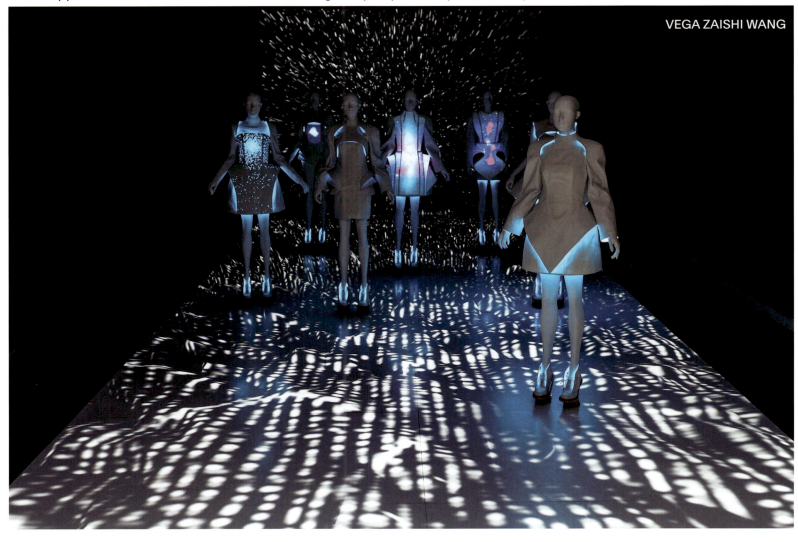

VEGA ZAISHI WANG

OLGA
NORONHA

AURORA BUREALIS

LEONID
TITOW

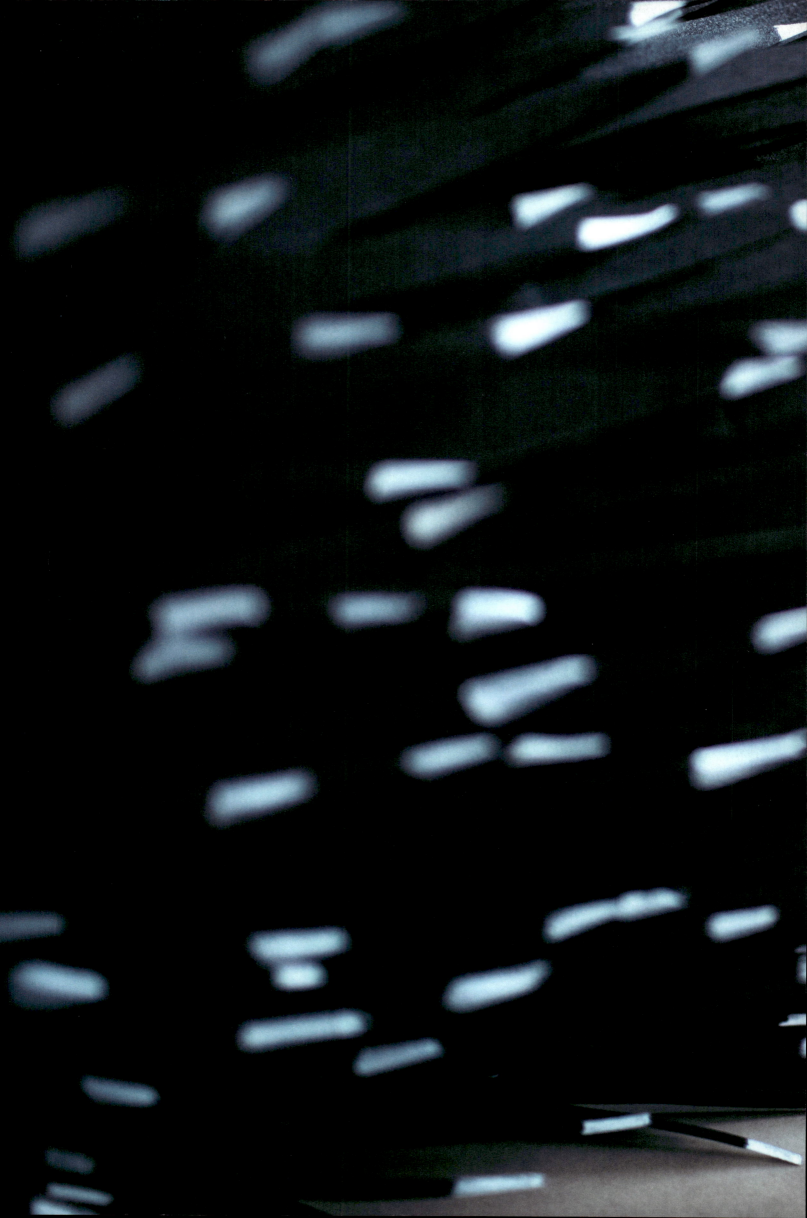

OTHERWORLDLY

Avant-Garde Fashion and Style

This book was conceived, edited, and designed by Gestalten.

Edited by Theo-Mass Lexileictous, Robert Klanten, and Sven Ehmann

Foreword by Greg French (PP. 1 – 8)
Texts by Theo-Mass Lexileictous (PP. 108 – 111, 283 – 289) and Greg French
(PP. 17 – 19, 69 – 71, 143 – 145, 189 – 191, 235 – 237)

Editorial management by Vanessa Obrecht
Copy-editing by Kevin Brochet-Nguyen
Proofreading by Ben Barlow
Theo-Mass's Studio: Aphrodite Koupepidou, Annie Markitanis

Layout by Floyd E. Schulze
Cover by Ludwig Wendt
Typefaces: Knif Mono by Axel Pelletanche Thévenart with Building Paris,
Plain by François Rappo

Cover photography by Mardiana Sani for Nixi Killick

Printed by Nino Druck GmbH, Neustadt/Weinstr.
Made in Germany

Published by Gestalten, Berlin 2016
ISBN: 978-3-89955-638-4

For more information, please visit www.gestalten.com.

Bibliographic information published by the Deutsche Nationalbibliothek.
The Deutsche Nationalbibliothek lists this publication in the Deutsche Nationalbibliografie;
detailed bibliographic data are available online at http://dnb.d-nb.de.

None of the content in this book was published in exchange for payment by commercial parties or designers;
Gestalten selected all included work based solely on its artistic merit.

This book was printed on FSC® certified paper.